RURAL ENTERPRISE IN KENYA

Development and Spatial Organization of the Nonfarm Sector

by
Donald B. Freeman
and
Glen B. Norcliffe
York University

THE UNIVERSITY OF CHICAGO
DEPARTMENT OF GEOGRAPHY
RESEARCH PAPER NO. 214

1985

Library of Congress Cataloging in Publication Data

Freeman, Donald B.
    Rural enterprise in Kenya.

    (Research paper / the University of Chicago, Department
of Geography ; no. 214)
    Bibliography: p. 171.
    1. Informal sector (Economics)--Kenya. 2. Rural
development--Kenya. I. Norcliffe, G. B. II. Title.
III. Series: Research paper (University of Chicago.
Dept. of Geography) ; no. 214.
H31.C514 no. 214   910 s   85-1037
[HD2346.K4]   [381]
ISBN 0-89065-119-1

Research Papers are available from:
The University of Chicago
The Department of Geography
5828 S. University Avenue
Chicago, Illinois 60637-1583
Price: $10.00; $7.50 by series subscription

CONTENTS

LIST OF ILLUSTRATIONS

LIST OF TABLES

viii

ACKNOWLEDGMENTS

This study is based on empirical data collected in rural Kenya in several detailed and extensive interview surveys. The survey of Central Province was carried out by a dedicated team of Kenyans, Messrs. Gathure, Mugo, Ndirangu, and Waithuki, and their supervisors Messrs. Chris Kureneri and Nicholas Miles. This team spent long periods in the field, working often in remote areas under difficult and even hazardous conditions. Other surveys were conducted by the staff of the Central Bureau of Statistics under the able direction of Messrs. Okoth Agunda and Parmeet Singh, assisted by John Kekovole and Ken Williams. We wish to express our sincere appreciation to the members of these teams for their hard work and their invaluable cooperation.

At the time of the surveys, both authors were attached to the Project Planning and Evaluation Unit within Kenya's Ministry of Economic Planning and Development and were encouraged in this research endeavor by Harris Mule, then Permanent Secretary of the Ministry. The helpful advice and guidance given by Dr. Mule and by officers in that Ministry did much to improve the design of the research and assure its completion. We also thank our colleagues on the York Kenya Project, especially its directors Tom Pinfold and John T. Saywell.

At York University, Toronto, are others to whom we owe our thanks. These include Charles Matthews, who assisted with computer programming; Hania Guzewska, Carolyn Gondor, and Carol Randall, who drew the illustrations; and Dawn Freeman, who, with assistance from Jane Crescenzi, worked wonders with a word processor to convert a very confused manuscript into a tidy final copy.

Financial assistance for this study was provided by the Canadian International Development Agency, which funded the Central Province Survey, and by the Social Sciences and Humanities Research Council of Canada, which provided sabbatical research funds for writing this study. This assistance is also gratefully acknowledged.

Given the institutional support we have received, it is important to stress that the positions taken and opinions stated in this monograph are those of the authors. They do not necessarily reflect the position of the individuals or institutions with whom we have worked. The authors assume full responsibility for any errors or shortcomings in this study.

Toronto, May 1983.

PREFACE

A decade ago, the International Labor Office published a study
entitled *Employment, Incomes and Equality* which focused on Kenya but
which, in retrospect, appears as a milestone in the analysis and
planning of all Third World economies.[1] A keynote of that
publication was its treatment of the informal or intermediate sector
of the economy, which is largely unregulated and unplanned,
consisting of petty commodity producers, traders, and service
workers. The authors of the ILO study pointed out that the
potential development role of this sector was profound, but that the
sector had, hitherto, been either ignored entirely or gravely
underestimated by planners and scholars dealing with Third World
development. Partly as a result of the ILO initiative, there has
been a growing interest in the informal sector in Kenya and
elsewhere, by researchers, by planners in the governments concerned,
and by international aid agencies.

Successive refinements of the concept of the informal sector
have included the drawing of distinctions between the urban informal
sector and the rural nonfarm sector by some researchers. Yet the
full importance of these distinctions between urban and rural
components is not being realized quickly enough, judging by the
number of studies still appearing that deal with "the" informal
sector. A preponderance of these studies really treat the urban
element, often without making very explicit their urban
orientation--while the much more extensive rural component has
received rather less attention. This lack of recognition of the
role of the rural nonfarm sector seems to be partly a consequence of
a persistent assumption among many social scientists that this
sector cannot be distinguished in any meaningful way from the urban
informal sector in its analytical and policy implications.
Admittedly, there are similarities in the nature of the urban and
rural sections of the informal sector. Both, for example, are
composed mainly of small, unregulated, lightly capitalized, and

---

1. International Labour Office, *Employment, Incomes and Equality* (Geneva:
ILO Publications, 1972).

strongly competitive enterprises, some of them part-time in nature. But to disregard the important functional differences between the two sectors because of these structural similarities is to risk choosing inappropriate development policies for both sectors.

As this study aims to demonstrate in detail, the rural nonfarm sector differs from the urban informal sector in three important ways. First, the rural nonfarm sector has its main relationships with peasant agriculture, particularly as regards markets, capital supply, labor, and a high proportion of raw material inputs. The urban informal sector, according to numerous studies, has its main relationships with the urban formal sector, often in the form of transnational corporations. Second, the nonfarm sector is primarily dispersed, being interwoven with the social and cultural as well as the economic fabric of rural areas. It is operated by rural residents whose social and commercial relationships bespeak continuity, a sense of belonging, and an orderly adjustment to changing opportunities. Employees in the urban informal sector, by contrast, are largely rural migrants. The majority are mostly young and landless men, who must operate in the often impersonal and even hostile milieu of the metropolis which herds and concentrates many informal activities into slums, exploits their laborers, and frequently subjects them to harassment and disruption. Third, the rural nonfarm sector is much larger than its urban counterpart in many Third World countries. In Kenya, for example, the rural nonfarm sector is fully eight times the size of the urban informal sector, in terms of numbers of people involved.

These characteristics, as we demonstrate in this study, cause the rural nonfarm sector to play a different role from its urban counterpart in the process of national development. In consequence, it should most definitely be dissociated from the urban informal sector when it comes to policy-making. Moreover, the negative criticism which some scholars have leveled at the urban informal sector is in many ways inapplicable to the rural nonfarm sector which, we will argue, should be viewed as an important part of the solution to the problems of Third World countries, in its role as an agent of rural consolidation.

Other critics have argued that the rural nonfarm sector, though presently flourishing, is a short-lived phenomenon: they claim that it is doomed to elimination in the Third World in the same way that small rural enterprises in the fairs and markets of Europe were eliminated by the Industrial Revolution and the urban dominance it generated. This forecast, based on comparative economic history of pre-industrial Europe and other regions, has also to be addressed in this study, since it implies that rural-oriented development policies may simply delay an inevitable--some may even say welcome--economic, spatial, and structural change in the Third World.

Such rural changes often came swiftly in nineteenth and early twentieth century Europe. To take a literary example, consider the opening scene of Thomas Hardy's classic novel, *The Mayor of Casterbridge,* describing Weydon-Priors fair which, for many generations, had been a major event in the life of rural Dorset. Hardy describes the market fair in the 1840s thus:

> The trusser and family . . . entered the Fair-field, which showed standing places and pens where many hundreds of horses and sheep had been exhibited and sold in the forenoon . . . the crowd was denser now than during the morning hours, the frivolous contingent of visitors, including journey-men out for a holiday, . . . village shopkeepers and the like, having latterly flocked in: persons whose activities found a congenial field among the peep-shows, toy-stands, waxworks, inspired monsters, disinterested medical men who travelled for the public good, thimbleriggers, nick-nack vendors, and readers of Fate.'2

When the central characters return eighteen years later, with the industrial revolution well on its way, a very different picture emerges. Weydon Fair is a pale shadow of its former self:

> Reaching the outskirts of the village . . . they ascended to the fair. Here, too, it was evident that the years had told. Certain mechanical improvements might have been noticed in the roundabouts and highfliers, machines for testing rustic strength and weights, and in the erections devoted to shooting for nuts. But the real business of the fair had considerably dwindled . . . neighbouring towns were beginning to interfere seriously with the trade carried on here for centuries. The pens of sheep, the tie-ropes for horses, were about half as long as they had been. The stalls of tailors, hosiers, coopers, linen-drapers, and other such trades had almost disappeared, and the vehicles were far less numerous.'3

This vignette from the early industrial European nonfarm sector does bear a strong similarity to examples from Africa over the past hundred years or more. Consider the following description of a West African market place filled with nonfarm enterprises. The English explorer Richard Lander visited this market, Rabba on the Niger river, in 1830. He found that:

> Rabba (is) considerably large, neat, clean, and well-built . . . It is irregularly built on the slope of a gently-rising hill, at the foot of which runs the Niger . . . It is inhabited by a mixed population . . . The arabs and all strangers have an enclosure of dwellings to themselves . . . Rabba is famous for milk, oil, and honey. The market, when our messengers were there, appeared to be well supplied with bullocks, horses, mules, asses, sheep, goats, and abundance of poultry. Rice and various sorts of corn, cotton, cloth, indigo, saddles and bridles made of red and yellow leather besides shoes, boots, and sandals, were offered for sale in great plenty . . . Although (the messengers) observed about two hundred slaves for sale, none had been

---

2. Thomas Hardy, *The Mayor of Casterbridge* (London: Smith Elder, 1886), pp. 3-4.

3. Ibid., p. 16.

disposed of when they left the market in the evening . . . The people
(of the area) are extremely industrious . . . In our walks we see groups
of people employed in spinning cotton and silk; others in making wooden
bowls and dishes, mats of various patterns, shoes, sandals, cotton
dresses and caps, and the like; others busily occupied in fashioning
brass and iron stirrups, bits for bridles, hoes, chains, fetters, &c.;
and others again employed in making saddles and horse accoutrements.
These various articles, which are intended for the Rabba market, evince
considerable taste and ingenuity in their execution."[4]

Lander's description of Rabba market catches the flavor of
even late twentieth century African markets (with some obvious
differences). But, bearing in mind the point of comparing these
vignettes of the European and African case examples, we are led to
ask: Is the rural nonfarm sector in tropical Africa destined to
fade like its early-industrial European counterparts? Or does it
still exhibit the vitality, prosperity, and signs of growth that
denote a viable future? Are such comparisons between contemporary
African nonfarm enterprises and long-dead European examples not
invalidated in any case by the existence of hidden differences that
underlie the (possibly superficial) similarities?

Questions of the role of the rural nonfarm sector, its
distinctiveness from the urban informal sector, its enduring or
ephemeral nature, and its proper treatment in development theory and
policy can only be answered when more detailed empirical knowledge
has been presented, placed in a theoretical context, analyzed, and
interpreted. This study attempts to contribute to these tasks. But
it goes further in response to the challenge presented by the
important problems of rural development in Africa and argues the
case for a more prominent position of the rural nonfarm sector in
policies for development of Third World rural regions, using Kenya
as a detailed example.

In chapter 1 we debate the theoretical questions concerning
the future of the rural nonfarm sector. Chapter 2 treats the
historical aspects of the sector's formation, and chapter 3 gives an
overview of its structure at the national level in Kenya, based on
empirical survey data. Chapter 4 delves in considerable detail into
the operation of the nonfarm enterprise in rural markets, using a
regional case example. Chapters 5 and 6 analyze the intersectoral
relationships of nonfarm activities, notably those with resources
and agriculture, and with urban firms, consumers, and the public
sector. Chapter 7 offers a synthesis of major findings, sets these
into a policy framework that emphasizes positive development of
rural nonfarm activities, and, we feel, vindicates our optimism with
regard to the developmental value of this sector.

---

4. Richard and John Lander, *Journal of an Expedition to Explore the Course
and Termination of the Niger,* 2 vols. (New York: J. and J. Harper, 1832), vol. 2,
pp. 82-85.

CHAPTER I

A RELIC OR AN EMBRYO? CHANGING VIEWPOINTS ON THE ROLE OF THE NONFARM SECTOR IN RURAL DEVELOPMENT

It is abundantly clear, especially to those who live there, that times are increasingly hard in countries such as Kenya that exist on the periphery of an international economy staggering under the afflictions of a prolonged recession. The World Bank has grimly forecast that the rest of this century will witness continued and widespread poverty, joblessness, and sluggish or declining productivity in the Third World, especially in low-income, oil-importing countries, unless there is a dramatic turn-around in basic indicators.[1] It is within this gloomy framework that all concerned with the rural areas in the Third World have been reappraising the tasks ahead, the available tools to deal with them, and the prospects for success. Development specialists are increasingly questioning and often rejecting stock development prescriptions from the past. As part of this process, the "informal sector," which includes the rural nonfarm sector, is receiving more attention.

In this chapter, we consider the rural nonfarm sector from this broader perspective of development theory. We bring to bear a particular concern with spatial implications of development. This involves explaining the way in which the nonfarm sector is viewed in past and present development theories and ideologies. A brief review of current scholarly understanding will set the stage for a description of the sector, an analysis of its role, and consideration on its development potential. We begin with a treatment of the standard neoclassical "modernization" paradigm that underlay the Western approach to development up to the early 1970s.[2]

---

1. World Bank, *World Development Report 1981* (Washington: The World Bank, 1981), pp. 17-18, 26-28.

2. Progressive modernization, the Western prescription for the Third World in the 1960s and early 1970s, focused on rapid industrial growth and the expansion of large-scale commercial agriculture, spurred on by incentives to the "saving classes" (indigenous capitalists and expatriate investors). It also involved the infusion of transnational capital in the form of public or private foreign borrowings and technology transfers suited to Western production modes. It thus focused almost exclusively on expansion of the formal sectors of Third World economies. In the view of many critics, however, it failed to provide meaningful improvement in living standards for the majority of Third World peoples over the last two decades. Some reasons are: (1) it led to excessive concentration of the means of production and the benefits of growth in the hands of an elite that was

1

The strong negative reaction to this perspective on the Third World
and its growth prospects embodied in the dependency paradigm will
then be outlined, as a point of departure for consideration of
recent post-dependency perspectives on rural development in the
Third World. These embrace both radical and reformist strategies.
It will become clear that attitudes to the rural nonfarm sector as
dealt with in these paradigms have changed to give the informal
sector a more prominent and helpful role.

Treatment of Nonfarm Activities under Neoclassical Economic Growth Models and the Spatial Modernization Paradigm

Neoclassical economic models of development have tended to
focus on growth of the formal sector, and especially on
industrialization and export expansion, as the key issues in
developing countries.[3] The informal sector, in contrast, has not
received serious attention in most growth models. Early two-sector
economic models usually viewed developing economies in terms of a
traditional agricultural sector and a modern industrial-commercial
sector, with the latter holding the real potential for growth.
Agriculture, however, was expected to bear the brunt of the
adjustments, including net capital and labor transfers, which were
deemed necessary for growth.[4] The rural nonfarm sector, when it was
considered at all, was regarded as a form of disguised unemployment[5]
and, being seen as part of the traditional sector, it was expected
to be eliminated as quickly as possible so that its role could be
assumed by modern urban firms.[6] Influential later models of the

---

mostly urban-based but which also controlled land ownership in rural areas; (2) it
led to wholesale export of scarce capital from poor countries via repatriated
profits and royalties to large transnational investors who in many cases had
raised much of their initial capital in the host country; (3) it involved
industrialization via import substitution in a context where commercial markets
were insufficiently developed to absorb "staple" manufactures, so that luxury
items were mostly produced, with the urban elites and the transnational
entrepreneurs as the main beneficiaries; (4) in some countries at least, it led to
establishment of monopolies, as "infant industry" arguments were used to obtain
protective legislation, thereby raising prices of goods to rural consumers and
undermining any increases in returns on commercial crops the latter may have
achieved; (5) there was an absence of the "trickle down" effects of urban
investments into rural peripheries, leading to increased urban-rural disparities
in standards of living; (6) many Third World countries that did succeed in
developing export-oriented manufacturing sectors found that their chief market
(the Western countries whose advisers had urged industrialization as the proper
course to follow) was constrained and often closed entirely by non-tariff barriers
and other restrictions designed to protect domestic Western producers, who could
not otherwise compete with labor-intensive Third World manufactures.

3. Douglas C. North, "Location Theory and Economic Growth" in *Regional
Development and Planning* ed. J. Friedmann and W. Alonso (Cambridge, Mass: M.I.T.
Press, 1964), pp. 248-249.

4. W.A. Lewis, "Economic Development with Unlimited Supplies of Labor," in
The Economics of Underdevelopment, ed. A.N. Agarwala and S.P. Singh (New York:
Oxford University Press, 1958); Ragnar Nurkse, *Problems of Capital Formation in
Underdeveloped Countries* (Oxford: Blackwell, 1957).

5. Benjamin Higgins, *Economic Development,* revised ed. (New York: W.W.
Norton, 1968), pp. 318-324.

6. J.C.H. Fei and G. Ranis, *Development of the Labor Surplus Economy*

"dual economy" saw the traditional sector, including the rural nonfarm sector, as essentially static and isolated, contributing virtually nothing to the development of the modern economy in Third World countries. This interpretation led to calls for a "big push" by foreign aid agencies to eliminate these traditional "bottlenecks."[7] In short, the prevailing view was that the traditional non-agricultural sector had value only as a labor pool, to be drawn down as needed by modern industry.[8]

The modernization paradigm of spatial economic development in the Third World was based on the above model of the structure of developing economies and their intersectoral relations. This was the conceptual platform on which diffusionist spatial models of "development" were erected in the 1960s and early 1970s.[9] These models proposed that innovation diffusion from the West was a desirable and even inevitable mechanism for Third World development and would naturally utilize the urban system of the host country for transmission of modern technology and innovative ideas.[10] Where urban centers that could fulfill this modernizing role did not exist, they must be created, providing "growth centers" through which modernizing influences and economic benefits of growth could "filter down" to the rural peripheries of these urban "cores."[11] Again, the rural nonfarm sector had no real place in these models.

Drawbacks of the modernization paradigm soon made themselves felt. The major disadvantages were that: (1) the paradigm is based on unrealistic assumptions about the processes of capital formation and technological transfer; thus, Schumpeterian concepts of intermittent invention and innovation do not apply, and, moreover, transnational monopoly capitalism has distorted the process of Third World industrialization;[12] (2) the paradigm ignores the realities of

---

(Homewood, Ill: Irwin, 1954).

7 . Benjamin Higgins, op. cit., pp. 265-266.

8 . Gunnar Myrdal, *Asian Drama: An Inquiry into the Poverty of Nations.* (New York: Parthenon Press, 1968), vol. 2, pp. 1156-57; Harold Brookfield, *Interdependent Development* (London: Methuen, 1975) pp. 54-62.

9 . L.E. Brown, *Innovation Diffusion: A New Perspective* (London and New York: Metheun, 1981).

10 . J. Barry Riddell, "Modernization in Sierra Leone," in *Contemporary Africa: Geography and Change,* ed. C. Gregory Knight and James L. Newman. (Englewood Cliffs: Prentice Hall, 1976), pp. 393-407.

11 . Edward W. Soja, *The Geography of Modernization in Kenya* (Syracuse: Syracuse University Press, 1968); Peter Gould, *Spatial Diffusion,* Resource Paper Series, (Washington: Association of American Geographers, 1969); Brian J.L. Berry, "Hierarchical Diffusion: The Basis of Developmental Filtering and Spread in a System of Growth Centers," in *Growth Centers in Regional Economic Development,* ed. Niles M. Hansen (New York: The Free Press, 1972); John Friedman, "A General Theory of Polarized Development" in *Growth Centers in Regional Economic Development.*

12 . L. Brown, op. cit., p. 181; Colin Leys, *Underdevelopment in Kenya: The Political Economy of Neo-Colonialism: 1964-1971* (London: Heinemann, 1975), pp. 8-9.

the political, social, and economic environments in underdeveloped
countries, particularly the growth of comprador elites who can
curtail the diffusion process; and (3) the paradigm has given
concrete evidence in some countries of exacerbating rather than
relieving the problems of underdevelopment.[13] The results of these
problems with modernization, convincingly demonstrated in the
critical literature, were that the rural poor in the Third World
were relatively (and in many cases absolutely) worse off than before
and that some Third World countries were ensnared in a trade system
where the terms of trade moved inexorably against them. Debt
service burdens mounted as the international loans used for
industrialization came due for repayment. Rural-to-urban migration
of landless rural workers increased, but urban jobs for them were
scarce.

The space-economies of Third World countries have gradually
changed to reflect these consequences of the modernization paradigm.
Geographic aspects include growing spatial polarity and urban
primacy, as innovation, capital, and technology have become
concentrated in the metropolitan urban core. This has adversely
affected rural areas, exacerbating the rural outmigration of skilled
labor, the sub-marginalization of small farmers, and the rise of
large land-owners in areas well-connected to the urban core. There
have been increasing regional inequities in services, incomes, and
productivity. These have left their stamp on the character of the
rural nonfarm sector.

The Rural Nonfarm Sector and the Dependency Perspective

The widespread negative reaction to the modernization paradigm
in the 1970s was initiated by scholars in what Brookfield has termed
the "periphery" of development study:[14] in other words, by those who
styled themselves as radicals, but also by neo-Marxist scholars in
Latin America and elsewhere. Those who adopted this dependency
perspective[15] claimed that the Third World was being actively

---

13 . J. Samuel Valenzuela and Arturo Valenzuela, "Modernization and
Dependence: Alternative Perspectives in the Study of Latin American
Underdevelopment," in *Transnational Capitalism and National Development,* ed. Jose
J. Villamil (Sussex: The Harvester Press, 1979), pp. 31-66.

14 . Harold Brookfield, *Interdependent Development* (London: Methuen, 1975),
p. 124.

15 . Dependency has been characterized as a perspective rather than a theory
by recent influential writers in the field who themselves espouse this point of
view, for example, by Valenzuela and Valenzuela. The same authors note that
dependency is largely a Marxist derivative. Others, such as Seers, however, see
modernization and Marxist approaches to development as being identical in the
sense that both focus on the objective of increasing productive capacity, whether
through capital accumulation by a saving class of entrepreneurs or through
redistribution of property rights (the "means of production" in Marxist parlance),

underdeveloped by the process of capital penetration of the newly
independent countries, and by their dependence on the West for
markets, technology, skills, and financial aid for modernization
programs.[16] The rural nonfarm sector is given short shrift in the
writings of many dependency perspective advocates. Often this is
because these writers have lumped the urban and rural elements of
the informal sector together and, so to speak, tarred them both with
the same brush. Colin Leys, for example, denigrates the informal
sector as "a system of very intense exploitation of labor."[17] He
adds that "what the 'informal sector' does is to provide the 'formal
sector' with goods and services at a very low price, which makes
possible the high profits of the 'formal sector'."[18] Leys
believes--erroneously, according to data in this study--that
informal sector workers are predominantly wage-workers (in fact, in
Kenya at least, most are self-employed).[19]

These viewpoints are enlarged upon by Godfrey and Langdon in a
quote that typifies the dependency perspective on informal
enterprises and its blurring of urban and rural elements of the
informal sector:

> 'Marginalization' does seem to result for many Kenyans--with many rural
> households squeezed on to plots that are too small for cash-crop
> production, while increased migration interacts, Latin American style,
> with growing unemployment and widespread unregulated indigenous
> enterprise in urban areas (as the ILO Report describes in detail). The
> resulting informal sector is structurally marginal to the economy in
> that it supplies only residual markets in which formal sector firms are
> not interested--as soon as small producers have developed a market to
> the extent that it is of interest, than [sic] large firms take it over
> (as happened recently to small-scale food kiosks in Nairobi). Burdened
> with very poor infrastructure, generating very low wages for its
> employees, often harassed by government, and characterized by highly
> competitive price-cutting, informal sector enterprise serves mainly to
> further surplus accumulation in the formal sector, by supplying very
> cheap products to firms and to wage employees in that sector.[20]

and both advocate the removal of obstacles to growth such as traditional or
religious practices, kinship ties or linguistic rigidities and barriers. In one
case the mechanism to bring about the above objective is "trickle down," in the
other case it is revolution. Consequently Seers labels this scenario the
"Chicago-Marxist Paradigm." See: J.S. Valenzuela and A. Valenzuela, op. cit., pp.
43 and 53; and also Dudley Seers, "Patterns of Dependence" in Jose Villamil, op.
cit., p. 96.

16. Andre Gunder Frank, *Capitalism and Underdevelopment in Latin America:
Historical Studies in Chile and Brazil,* rev. ed. (New York: Monthly Review Press,
1969).

17. Colin Leys, op. cit., p. 267.

18. Ibid.

19. Ibid. Contrast Leys' statement with empirically based findings in this
study relating to the rural sector (which is much larger than the urban sector)
and also with the data and viewpoints presented in: William House, "Nairobi's
Informal Sector," in *Papers on the Kenyan Economy,* ed. Tony Killick (Nairobi:
Heinemann, 1981), pp. 357-368.

20. Martin Godfrey and Steven Langdon, "Partners in Underdevelopment? The
Transnationalization Thesis in a Kenyan Context," in Jose Villamil, op. cit., p.
269.

This view of the informal or traditional sectors as being
marginal, exploited by and supportive of the modern capitalist
sector and worthy only of dissolution, so widely held among
dependency advocates, is not really any different from the viewpoint
of the neoclassical economists mentioned earlier. The noted
dependency theorist Tamas Szentes, for example, painted this stock
view of a dual economy in which the traditional sector is isolated,
stagnant, and in need of dissolution in order to effect progress.[21]
He, like numbers of other dependency theorists, is given to
unsupported generalizations about the sector (for example its
alleged propensity to total consumption and its supposed
preponderance of wage employees). These ideas are certainly not
borne out by empirical evidence in Kenya.

Among the early critics of the prevailing spatial or
geographical modernization approaches, Logan,[22] Brookfield,[23]
Slater,[24] and de Souza and Porter[25] all voiced misgivings that the
spatial modernization paradigm could not clarify the processes
underlying the geographic patterns which were the primary focus of
the geographers' development models. The arguments of the
dependency school regarding the inadequacies of spatial models were
made forcefully by Goodenough[26] and Ettema[27] who urged greater
sensitivity to the effects of (neo)colonialism on Third World
societies and who declared the need to reconsider the conceptual
basis of geographic study of the Third World. In turn, the
dependency perspectives were criticized for failing to provide a
positive basis for future geographic approaches to the study of
development issues.[28] There is no doubt, however, that the criticism
of modernization by the dependency theorists was a timely and

21. Tamas Szentes, *The Political Economy of Underdevelopment* (Budapest: Akademiai Kiado, 1971), p. 249.

22. M.I. Logan, "The Development Process in the Less Developed Countries," *Australian Geographer* 12 (1972): 146-153.

23. Harold Brookfield, op. cit.

24. David Slater, "Geography and Underdevelopment" *Antipode* 5, no. 3 (1973), pp. 21-33.

25. A.R. de Souza and P.W. Porter, *The Underdevelopment and Modernization of the Third World,* Resource Paper no. 28 (Washington, D.C: Association of American Geographers, Commission on College Geography, 1974).

26. Stephanie Goodenough, *Values, Relevance and Ideology in Third World Geography* (Milton Keynes: Open University Press, 1977).

27. W.A. Ettema, "Geographers and Development" *Tijdschrift voor Economische en Sociale Geografie,* 40 (1979): 66-74.

28. Donald B. Freeman, *The Geography of Development and Modernization: A Survey of Present Trends and Future Prospects,* Discussion Paper no. 22 (Toronto: York University Department of Geography, 1979); J.G. Browett, "On the Role of Geography in Development Geography," *Tijdschrift voor Economische en Sociale Geografie,* 72 (1981): 155-161.

valuable exercise. But the task yet to be done is the rebuilding of valid models--economic, social, and geographical--of development processes that have pragmatic worth as well as theoretical integrity.

Post-Dependency Approaches to Rural Development and Nonfarm Activities

Following the modernization-dependency debate, development studies seem now to be moving toward the goal of recasting theoretical underpinnings, with the aid of concepts derived from various social sciences, the better to contribute to the solution of problems and disorders attendant on the struggle for development in the Third World. Yet, the approaches advocated continue on different paths, leading to an on-going dialectic. While it would be preferable to stress the communalities and areas of accord in the study of development, we concede that different world views and ideologies involved in the continuing dialectic presage two separate analytical streams that are making their appearance in the wake of the dependency debate. These have been characterized by some researchers as the radical approach and the approach of reformism. Other scholars have tried to schematize the various schools of "liberal" and "radical" theory.[29] These epithets refer more, however, to the sentiment of the researchers than to the actual programs and models proposed. We prefer to postulate the existence of a continuum between revolutionary paradigms and paradigms of gradualism, along which previous studies are arranged in rather clustered fashion. Perhaps most recent studies are clustered nearer to the "revolutionary" end of the spectrum, but with some "basic needs" or "reformist" models closer to the "gradualist" end. In discussing specific examples, we focus, as is appropriate in this study, on works that have bearing on rural-informal activities and/or emphasize spatial or geographical aspects.

Revolutionary, Spatial Development Approaches

Radical scholars frequently complain that "mainstream" colleagues divorce spatial from social process and structure, which many of them clearly see as the appropriate focus of analysis. This is especially true of many orthodox Marxists, whose dislike of "the fetishism of space" leads them to relegate spatial analysis to an insignificant role and to view their scholarly disciplines as a forum for revolutionary doctrine, or simply as a stepping stone to a

---

29 . A. de Souza, "Commentary: Dialectic Development Geography," *Tijdschrift voor Economische en Sociale Geografie* 73 (1982): 122-128; J.G. Browett, op. cit.; P.J. Rimmer and D.K. Forbers, "Underdevelopment Theory: A Geographical Review," *Australian Geographer* 15 (November 1982): 197-210.

8

"critical social theory."[30] Among radical geographers, four main themes have been the study of unequal spatial development, urban modes of production, peasant mobility, and urban "goods" such as housing and medicine.[31]

Spatial analysis of conditions in non-agricultural rural sectors is not a significant feature of revolutionary writings. The assumption is clearly that political-structural reorientation at the state level will "take care of" problems of rural development as part of a general reshaping of society. The expectation, either explicit or implicit in some radical writings, that the overthrow of existing regimes in the Third World and removal of ties with the West will bring about rapid material and social improvement for the rural masses has utopian appeal. Mounting experience suggests, however, that this may very well lead to a compounding of mistakes and to even greater wholesale misery for many rural peoples in the Third World. Real and lasting improvements in living conditions among peripheral peoples certainly require rapid and profound changes to be brought about, both within the regions affected and within the international community. But it is not enough to suggest, as some have done, that replacement of the political apparatus to eliminate capitalist modes of production will in itself solve problems of spatial inequality and rural deprivation.

Revolutionary scholars would be well advised to work to change public and political attitudes to the Third World in the United States and other developed countries, as de Souza notes.[32] Within developing countries themselves, meanwhile, there is much that can be (and is being) done to influence decision makers and planners and to bring about meaningful change toward lasting improvement without destructive confrontation and conflict. These initiatives include the adoption of less radical solutions, such as basic needs approaches, rural reformism, and others closer to the gradualist end of the spectrum.

8

---

30. J. Lewis, *Ideology and the Geography of Development* (paper prepared for the Anglo-French Symposium on Ideology and Geography, March 23-25, 1979). Some scholars with strong radical convictions appear to be advocating for themselves and others the abandonment of scholarly approaches altogether in favor of political activism: " . . . Marxists insist that geographers give up their elitist role because they cannot appreciate the sacrifices others must make and because revolutionary theory cannot be developed in isolation from revolutionary practice." A. de Souza, op. cit., p. 124.

31. P.J. Rimmer and D.K. Forbes, op. cit., p. 205.

32. A. de Souza, op. cit., p. 125.

Basic Needs Approaches to Rural Development

Among many students of development problems there is a conviction that neither the progressive modernization nor the revolutionary Marxist, neo-Marxist, or Radical-Social approaches are suited to the types of societies and environments in many Third World countries. Some scholars believe also that elimination of ties with the West inevitably would lead to dependence of a different sort, perhaps with the Soviet Union playing the role now played by Western countries. The dangers of being locked into any sort of international bloc has led to promulgation of collective self-reliance strategies, "basic needs prescriptions," or other gradualist approaches to development problems. It would not, however, be accurate to dismiss these ideas (as some have done) simply as arguments in favor of the status quo or as conservative or retreatist positions, since such strategies aim to bring about profound changes in the space-economies of developing nations. The critical point is that they seek to do this without wholesale conflict.

One of the first researchers to outline the features of a basic needs approach to development was Paul Streeten.[33] He points out that this approach covers a broad range of strategies that concentrate on achieving the particular ends of alleviating poverty and meeting material needs of the rural and urban poor. The relevance of this approach for the rural nonfarm sector in Third World countries is direct and immediate. First, the strategy would aim to achieve its goals largely through contact with rural masses via channels where nonfarm activities have a major role to play, as in small rural market centers. Second, public services such as health, education, and family planning aids need to be combined with other, privately-provided services such as transport, clothing, and food supply (which are mostly obtained through the rural nonfarm sector).

Poverty alleviation and basic needs fulfilment were actually adopted as the central theme in Kenya's 1979-83 Development Plan.[34] In that strategy, however, the primary focus was on public services, although ancillary policies to stimulate the rural nonfarm sector have also been drafted, if not yet fully implemented.

---

33. Paul Streeten, "The Distinctive Features of a Basic Needs Approach to Development," *International Development Review* 19 (1977): 8-16.

34. Martin Godfrey, "Basic Needs and Planning in Kenya," in *Models, Planning and Basic Needs,* ed. S. Cole and H. Lucas (Oxford: Pergamon Press, 1979), pp. 51-59.

10

As so far developed, the Kenyan basic needs approach tends to be strongly pragmatic, but not without a basis in theory. Like other similar approaches, it operates on an assumption that real and lasting changes can be brought about within existing social and political structures, provided there is good will and a genuine desire for improvement on the part of decision-makers, at whom the strategy is directed. In the Kenyan case, the public sector is viewed as playing the leading role (through increasing expenditure on services and through stimulation of productive activities in the informal sector). The theory is that through their various linkages, the public and informal sectors are the most likely sectors to provide powerful impulses to pervasive industrialization, construction, agriculture, and services.[35] Stimulation of these key sectors will induce "a new dynamism in the economy" that should lead to removal of the most persistent form of poverty, that of the working poor in the rural areas.

The activities that qualify as "basic needs activities" must at least share these characteristics: (1) raise incomes of the poor through creation of employment and increasing productivity of those now employed; (2) contribute to the satisfaction of "core" needs such as nutrition, health, education, housing, and water; (3) increase production of other basic goods and services (what we shall term *household needs*) such as food, textiles, shoes, utensils, furniture, and personal effects bought in the small markets by low-income groups; (4) enhance decentralization, participation and self reliance.[36]

Given the objectives and underlying concepts of the basic needs approach, it is not surprising that the rural nonfarm sector, as a major element of the informal sector, is regarded as a central and crucial part of this development paradigm. Indeed, its role is discussed at length by Ghai et al. in the detailed report setting out their pioneering conceptual framework.[37] They say specifically that Government must stimulate agroprocessing, construction, and service activities that are part of this sector.[38]

35. Republic of Kenya, Ministry of Economic Planning and Development, *Alleviating Poverty and Meeting Basic Human Needs in Kenya* (Nairobi, 1977), p. 4. Mimeograph.

36. D. Ghai, M. Thorbecke, and M. Godfrey, *Alleviating Poverty and Meeting Basic Human Needs in Kenya: Report of an ILO Consultancy Mission* (Nairobi, 1977), pp. 35-36. Mimeograph.

37. Ibid., pp. 39-44.

38. Republic of Kenya, *Alleviating Poverty,* p. 9.

More recently, some researchers have introduced refinements into the definition of "basic needs." John Friedmann, for example, identifies a general category of *human needs* or survival needs, *social needs* (transportation and tertiary education, for example), and *individual needs*.[39] The roles of the urban and rural informal sectors in the basic needs strategy have also been developed by William House[40] and by Norcliffe, Freeman, and Miles.[41]

Rural Reorganization

Other approaches to the development of the Third World which display varying degrees of concern for rural reorganization and development of the nonfarm sector include the "redistribution from growth" concept of the World Bank which has led to the work on rural development by Rondinelli and Ruddle, and specifically on rural industrialization by Anderson and Lieserson.[42] These approaches retain the notion of growth in the economy as a goal in itself, and do not see an incompatibility between urban growth and rural welfare, but rather a mutually supportive relationship in Third World countries.

The contribution of Akin Mabogunje[43] to the analysis of rural spatial reorganization and development has also been an important one. As Mabogunje points out, land reform programes are an essential prerequisite for genuine rural reorganization which has as its objective "to rescue the farming population from the contradictions of operating in a modern industrialized economy with means, institutions, organizations and rules of a traditional pre-industrial society."[44] Land reform not only involved reapportionment, but also valorization--giving it new value--and conservation. The associated restructuring of rural settlement, as Mabogunje notes, has strong implications for rural nonfarm activities also, and this, in turn, has bearing on the question of societal behavior and decision-making in rural communities.

---

39. John Friedmann and C. Weaver, *Territory and Function: The Evolution of Regional Planning* (Berkeley and Los Angeles: University of California Press, 1979), p. 190.

40. William House, op. cit.

41. G.B. Norcliffe, D.B. Freeman, and N. Miles, *Policies for Rural Industrialization in Kenya,* Working Paper no. 1 (Geneva: International Labour Office Rural Industrialization Project, 1980).

42. Dennis A. Rondinelli and K. Ruddle, *Urbanization and Rural Development: A Spatial Policy for Equitable Growth* (New York: Praeger, 1978); D. Anderson and M.W. Lieserson, *Rural Enterprise and Nonfarm Employment* (Washington, D.C.: World Bank, 1978).

43. Akin Mabogunje, *The Development Process: A Spatial Perspective* (London: Hutchinson, 1980).

44. Ibid., p. 105.

Mabogunje clearly favors cooperative rather than individualistic decision frameworks for rural reorganization.[45] This will result in the selection of specific types of "basic needs" and the spatial systems devised to supply these needs. This approach addresses two critical issues with profound bearing on development of rural nonfarm--and farm--sectors: " . . . first, it (would) ensure meaningful participation of all citizens in productive activities; and second, it (would) keep the population in the rural areas until industrial development in the urban centers has grown to such a level as to be able to provide alternative employment without compromising the capacity of the rural areas to supply food and industrial raw materials."[46] As part of this approach, Mabogunje favors locating small-scale processing industries in small rural towns, after the pattern followed in nineteenth century Japan.[47]

Development Approaches Involving Regional Closure, Regional Self Reliance, and Ruralization

Alternative development solutions include: promoting collective self-reliance, increasing cooperation among Third World nations in food production, and sharing of technology and education. The basic self-reliant model of growth, as advocated by Samir Amin,[48] Enrique Otieza[49] and others, entails: (1) satisfaction of the basic needs of the population, (2) disengagement from the world capitalist economy, (3) massive redistribution of income and wealth, (4) greater collaboration among Third World countries, and (5) the assumption by the State of much greater control over the means of production. "Delinking" from the international community entirely is not, however, necessary for collective self-reliance. But there would need to be deemphasizing of export cash crops such as coffee, tea, and fibers, which go to the developed West, and an increasing emphasis on domestic food crops.[50]

Collective self-reliance and delinking would not, however, help the situation within Third World countries where strong urban-rural disparities already exist, where the metropolis (often a primate city) and its region dominate other regions, and where the

---

45. Ibid., p. 113.

46. Ibid., p. 116.

47. Ibid., p. 212.

48. Samir Amin, "Le modèle théorétique d'accumulation et de développement dans le monde contemporain. La problématique de transition," *Tiers Monde* 12 (1972): 10-12.

49. Enrique Otieza, "Collective Self-Reliance: Some Old and New Issues," in *Transnational Capitalism and National Development,* ed. Jose Villamil (Sussex: The Harvester Press, 1979), pp. 289-306.

50. Samir Amin, op. cit.

benefits of production are poorly spread among regions or classes. Development, as Seers rightly notes, should be defined to include the reduction of political hegemony and of cultural dependence on one or a few of the great powers.[51] But the definition should also include reduction of regional disparities and dependency of the peripheral regions on the urban core. This brings us to the consideration of ruralization strategies and regional self-reliance.

Calls to increase regional self-reliance have been made by Friedmann and Douglass,[52] Stohr and Palme,[53] Freeman,[54] and Mabogunje.[55] The essence of these self-reliance or "partial regional closure" models is to reduce the backwash-inducing effects of linkages to the metropolises of the Third World countries and, through these, to the international economy. A network of central places linked into a hierarchical system of cities with their dependent hinterlands is patently the opposite of what regional self-reliance tries to bring about. The "core-periphery" model, featuring an industrialized metropole and a dependent rural hinterland, was the centerpiece of the modernization paradigm. As such, it brought about polarized development, featuring increasing regional disparities. The now-disfavored "redistribution from growth" ideas compatible with the core-periphery model basically relied on government-sponsored income transfers and filtering-down effects. These were expected to ameliorate disparities and render the affected space-economies politically viable and tolerable to the rural poor, who were being asked to underwrite this pattern of unequal development. Such is the nature of backwash processes in a core-periphery system, however, that redistribution of this sort would be no more effective than a band-aid on a steadily worsening rash of rural urban disparities, with the end result a swelling of the urban informal sector in the manner described in detail elsewhere.[56]

51. Dudley Seers, "The New Meaning of Development," *International Development Review* 19 (1977): p. 9.

52. John Friedmann and M. Douglass, "Regional Planning and Development: The Agropolitan Approach," in *Growth Pole Strategy and Regional Development Planning in Asia* (Nagoya: UNCRD, 1976), pp. 333-387.

53. W. Stohr and H. Palme, "Centre-Periphery Development Alternatives and their Applicability to Rural Areas in Developing Countries," Paper prepared for the ASA/LASA Joint Meetings, Houston, Texas, Sept. 1977.

54. D.B. Freeman, op. cit.

55. Akin Mabogunje, op. cit.

56. D.B. Freeman, op. cit.

Friedmann and Douglass put forward one of the most complete models of a space economy built on regional self-reliance yet devised. They consider theirs to be a "basic needs" approach,[57] where their definition of basic needs is "the sum of reciprocal claims in a territorially integrated society."[58] Their model has also been dubbed "cities in the fields" since it envisages that urban-style services can be delivered in a system of dispersed facilities located in rural areas (agropolitan districts) in order to serve a peasant hinterland without long distance travel by consumers of the services.

Friedmann considers that there are three conditions necessary for the success of his "agropolitan district" basic-need strategy:[59]

 1. Selective territorial closure, or enlightened self-reliance at "relevant" levels of territorial integration, either district, region, or nation. As Friedmann notes, this idea is contrary to the prevailing neoclassical notions of comparative advantage and free trade.[60]
 2. Communalization of productive wealth, or assertion of the priority interest of the community in the basic conditions of its sustenance. For many communities, this refers to communalized sharing of the wealth embodied in land and water resources.
 3. Equalization of access to the bases for the accumulation of social power. Friedmann holds the view that social power concentrated in a few hands leads to dominance-dependence relations rather than the freely cooperative relations which enhance voluntary increases in productive effort.

In the agropolitan district concept, a territorial framework is explicit. This framework arises as the result of the conjunction of three abstract spaces: cultural space, giving shared values and cultural understanding to the community; political space, the territorial manifestation of political institutions and criteria that guide and give formal identity to the community; and economic space, the interdependent productive activities and forces which are the basis of livelihood for the community. Agropolitan districts are, in Friedmann's model, the smallest spatial units that can provide the basic needs of the community without inordinate resource transfers from outside regions. Agropolitan districts are therefore

57 . Friedmann and Weaver, op. cit., p. 189.
58 . Ibid., p. 190.
59 . Ibid., pp. 194-195.
60 . See also D.B. Freeman, op. cit., pp. 26-27.

rural areas incorporating one or a few country towns and a rural
area with a population of between 20,000 and 100,000 distributed at
a density of at least 200 persons per square kilometer.

Development on the basis of agropolitan districts should, as
Friedmann notes, attempt to diversify the territorial economy,
should aim for maximum development of physical resources consistent
with principles of conservation, should be self-financed, and should
promote increased social education and the expansion of regional
markets.

Friedmann's model is but one of a number of recent strategies
which might be termed "ruralization" approaches since their
objective is to replace present trends toward urbanization and
industrial concentration in the Third World with alternative
frameworks that restore and reinforce rural economies, rural
lifestyles, and rural values. One of the most promising of these is
the so-called "maket raun" concept being applied by planners in
rural Papua-New Guinea.[61] This concept utilizes the system of market
rings, or spatially and temporally synchronized periodic markets
which have existed for centuries in many Third World countries.
This system replaces the more familiar central place hierarchy in
developed countries with one geared to the mobility pattern of
part-time traders and craftsmen, some of whom travel a circuit of
marketplaces each week and thereby bring high-order goods and
services to the peasant population. This frees peasants from the
requirement of travel over long distances to large towns in order to
obtain equivalent goods and services. Government services such as
health clinics, libraries, loan agencies, circuit courts, and adult
education teams can likewise be made "mobile" and follow the rings
of markets so as to be present at a particular market place on its
special market day(s) each week or month. This system of planned
"maket rauns" has importance for development of the rural nonfarm
sector--and for rural development generally--in the following ways:
(1) it provides for the basic needs of the rural poor closer to
where they live; (2) it reinforces the concept of regional closure
and greater territorial self-reliance, through the strengthening of
local market rings and the de-emphasizing of connections to a
dominant urban center or system of centers (that would otherwise
extend their hegemony over all aspects of rural life); (3) it

61. "Maket rauns," to use the pidgin-English term applied to these in
Papua-New Guinea, are essentially an artifact of government planners since
marketing is an introduced system of exchange in this region. See N. Clark, et
al., *Maket Raun: A Report to the Central Planning Office Papua-New Guinea* (1971)
Mimeograph. R.G. Ward, et al., *Growth Centres and Area Improvement in the Eastern
Highland District: A Report to the Central Planning Office, Papua-New Guinea*
(1974). Mimeograph.

ensures a sufficient "threshold" of consumers to the locationally
fixed, part-time vendors and the mobile enterprises, as well as to
the government services that travel the market rings, making the
system economically feasible; and (4) it retains jobs in the rural
areas rather than in the larger urban areas (as in the case of
standard Central Place systems).

The maket raun concept, however, looks only at one aspect of
rural development, that being the provision of household goods and
services not available on peasant farmsteads themselves. It does
not take direct account of other aspects such as basic food
production and resource conservation, and of nonmobile social
overhead installations such as rural energy supply. Some of these
aspects are dealt with in the concept of *ecodevelopment* put forward
by Ignacy Sachs.[62]

Ecodevelopment

This concept implies a form of development that is suited to
rural areas of the Third World, in which basic human needs (food,
housing, health, and education) are met, the quality of human social
relations maintained, and resources for the future managed so as to
minimize wastage and take advantage of environmental
complementarities. Ecodevelopment in the Third World requires the
use of appropriate technology, the adoption of suitable social
organization, and the revision of educational frameworks. It aims
to "create a durable equilibrium between man and nature, while
avoiding the errors of lawless growth." Like the models of Samir
Amin, Enrique Otieza, John Friedmann, and others, the notion of
ecodevelopment emphasizes self-reliance. It also has a regional or
territorial base in that it seeks specific solutions to regional
problems and tries to avoid both universal panaceas and extreme
ecologism.

Summary

At the beginning of this chapter, we asked rhetorically
whether the rural nonfarm sector has a place in future development
theory and strategy. The subsequent review of the way the sector
has been treated in the evolving neoclassical, Marxist, dependency,
and post-dependency schools of thought reveals that there is no
single unequivocal answer if one keeps to the literal
interpretations of the terms "rural development" and "informal
sector" in these various paradigms. Strategies of

---

62. Ignacy Sachs, "Ecodevelopment," *Ceres: The FAO Review on Agriculture and Development* ILII, (1974): 8-12.

government-imposed development (termed "top down" strategies) have
been mixed with grass-roots programs (known as "bottom up"
approaches) in various versions of all of the broad schools of
thought.[63] The overall impression, to echo the sentiments expressed
in a recent review of regional planning theory and strategy in rural
Africa,[64] is one of ever-changing viewpoints and planning
priorities.

But out of more than a decade of scholarly debate--some of it
quite acrimonious--a consensus seems to be emerging.[65] This is that
rural areas of the Third World, particularly in the low- income,
oil-importing countries, hold the key to the future development of
this entire world-region and that such advancement will only occur
if incentives and resources are given for local participation in
regional development. Freedom from overwhelming outside pressures,
such as are sometimes generated by transnational or large scale
urban capitalist enterprises that penetrate rural areas, is another
condition for rural development on which a general consensus seems
to be crystallizing. The importance of regional integrity and the
worth of appropriate technologies applied to agroprocessing, to
small-scale manufacturing, and to rural service industries is also
broadly acknowledged.

These areas of growing consensus are exactly the areas that
embrace the rural nonfarm sector; hence our belief that the nonfarm
sector has a positive role to play in development theory. The
specific aspects of this role, and the bearing it has on development
theory, are analyzed in the following chapters in which empirical
flesh is put on the theoretical bones briefly outlined above.

---

63 . W. Stohr and D.R.F. Taylor, *Development from Above or Below? A Radical
Reappraisal of Spatial Planning in Developing Countries* (New York: John Wiley,
1981).

64 . Assefa Mehretu and David J. Campbell, "Regional Planning for Small
Communities in Rural Africa: A Critical Survey," *Rural Africana* 12-13
(Winter-Spring 1981-82): 91-110.

65 . Ibid.

CHAPTER II

DEVELOPMENT OF THE RURAL NONFARM SECTOR IN KENYA: THREE FORMATIVE PERIODS

Current patterns and processes in Kenya's rural nonfarm sector are rooted in a long sequence of growth and change. This chapter surveys the course of events leading to the formation of the contemporary nonfarm sector. The discussion of this formative process will cover trading, marketing, service, and manufacturing activities in three distinct periods: the pre-colonial, colonial, and post-colonial eras. The analysis seeks to show that present patterns in the nonfarm sector are an outgrowth of combined European, Asian, and rural African influences.

Nonfarm Production and Trade in the Precolonial Period

It would be wrong to assume that trade and craft industries were absent from pre-colonial society in East Africa. Records reveal that both local and long-distance trade have a long history, although in the pre-colonial period the systems were, quite naturally, much simpler than those that evolved later. Craft industries, such as metal working, have been practiced for several centuries by many of the agricultural tribes and also, in a few instances, by pastoral groups.

Records of sightings of Mount Kilimanjaro and great lakes in the East African interior in *The Periplus of the Erythrean Sea* and in Ptolemy's *Geography* suggest that foreign commercial penetration of this region (probably for ivory) took place as early as the fourth century A.D. However, the scanty records suggest that thereafter, up until the eighteenth century, there was little long distance trade with the interior.[1] From the thirteenth to the fifteenth centuries, the Arab city states of the Coast enjoyed a period of considerable prosperity. High grade iron ore was mined and exported from Malindi and Mombasa, and these city states also exported slaves and ivory. The absence of exotic artifacts in interior archaeological sites dating to this period, however,

---

1. Roland Oliver and J.D. Fage, *A Short History of Africa* (Harmondsworth, Middlesex: Penguin, 1962), pp. 96-100.

suggests that, up to the eighteenth century, the trade of these city states was largely confined to the coastal strip of Kenya.

The Kamba Trading Region

In the late eighteenth century, long-distance trading between the coast and the interior expanded, and by the mid-nineteenth century, the Kamba peoples of east central Kenya were major participants in a trading network that stretched from the great lakes to the Swahili city states on the Indian Ocean coast. The Kamba were well placed to perform this "middleman" role between the slave and ivory ports along the coast and the pastoral and agricultural peoples in the remote interior who were especially in need of salt, iron, cloth, and luxury items.[2]

The Kamba, thus, traded with Masai, Kikuyu, and Meru peoples on their western borders and organized trading expeditions as far afield as Lake Tanganyika. The Kamba trading empire reached its zenith around 1840 but declined as Arab and Swahili traders, and later Asian (Indian) and European traders and explorers, pressed further into the interior, having gained the ability to cross hostile territories with their own trading caravans. Nevertheless, as a result of this trading experience, the Kamba maintained a commercial capability into the colonial period, albeit at a much reduced level.

The work of Lamphear indicates that, apart from the Kamba, Nyika tribes like the Giriama developed long distance caravans in response to the needs of the Swahili and Arab coastal towns. The Nyika retained the position of middlemen, so that only for a very short period did the Kamba actually trade directly with the Swahili towns. Long distance trade goods included ivory and gum copal, and probably slaves as well, although this is not mentioned in the context of Kamba trade. Nyika markets included Kwa Jomvu and Shongi.[3] In the latter part of the nineteenth century, forays by warlike bands of Masai, Galla, and Shambala halted much of the long-distance trade conducted by the Kamba and Nyika, forcing the Arabs to mount large, well armed caravans of their own into the interior.

---

2. John Lamphear, "The Kamba and the Northern Mrima Coast," in *Pre-Colonial African Trade,* ed. R. Gray and D. Birmingham (London: Oxford University Press, 1970), p. 101.

3. Ibid., p. 80.

Long Distance Trade among the Agricultural Bantu

In pre-colonial and early colonial times, several other groups developed trade linkages that foreshadowed the development of rural nonfarm enterprise systems in their regions. These included Bantu groups such as the Taita, Meru, and Gusii, and the non-Bantu Luo (previously called the Kavirondo).

The Taita participated in long distance trade in a passive rather than an active mercantile role. Instead of organizing their own caravan systems, they were content to allow Arab and Swahili caravans to use their homeland--protected as it was by forests and mountains--as a way station and provisioning post on the dangerous journeys across Masai lands. They naturally traded their own crafts (such as raffia basket work) and farm produce for cloth, beads, iron goods and other necessities carried by the caravans. They also permitted the recruiting of Taita men as porters, guides, interpreters, and guards for the ivory and slave caravans.[4]

The Meru peoples of the Nyambeni range and the north-east slopes of Mount Kenya were another Bantu group that developed long-distance trade functions prior to European colonization. They traded with surrounding pastoral groups to the north and west including the Laikipia Masai.[5] Once again, the Meru were to some extent middlemen for the coastal Arab and Swahili caravan operators. They exchanged with these caravans local produce including honey, beer, the narcotic herb miraa *(Catha edulis)*, crafts, donkeys, salt, and tobacco in return for wire, brass, beads, cloth, and cowrie shells.[6] This trade, as Bernard notes, "was not uncommon elsewhere in East Africa where Nilotic pastoralists and Bantu agriculturalists were adjacent. The technologial and ecological divergency of farming and pastoralism thus fostered complementarity and cooperation."[7]

Apart from indications of participation by the Meru in this long distance trade, however, evidence of commercial activity in the area suggests that barter exchange was quite sporadic and loosely organized. There are, nevertheless, a number of references by European explorers to the effect that several indigenous markets predate colonial times in the Nyambeni ranges.[8] It appears that in

---

4. Anne E. Frontera, *Persistance and Change: A History of Taveta* (Waltham, Mass: Crossroads Press, 1978), pp. 11-15.

5. Frank E. Bernard, "Meru District in the Kenyan Spatial Economy: 1890-1950," in *The Spatial Structure of Development: A Study of Kenya,* ed. R.A. Obudho and D.R.F. Taylor (Boulder, Colo: Westview Press, 1979), p. 266.

6. Ibid., p. 267

7. Ibid., p. 266.

the Nyambeni district, some regular markets were indeed held in open places where women traded in crafts and agricultural produce, and men in livestock.[9]

Local Trade

Similar fragmentary evidence records the existence of trading activities involving caravans and local periodic barter exchanges in other areas of Kenya, including Nyanza, where Luo and Gusii are reported to have engaged sporadically in such activities prior to colonial times.[10] Taylor claims that before colonial times, there was a "highly organized spatial system" of Kikuyu local markets in what is now Central Province. He says that exchange points existed between three ecological zones of the Kikuyu homeland: "high Kikuyu, middle Kikuyu, and low Kikuyu", with larger markets located so as to facilitate commerce in goods from all three zones.[11] Taylor identifies three types of markets: small, dealing with exchange in one ecological zone; larger markets, dealing with exchange between two different zones; and largest, dealing with exchange among all three types of zone. The latter were established in the middle Kikuyu ecological region. Taylor admits, however, that information on the evolution of these pre-colonial markets is scarce. Consequently, it is not clear how extensive these trading systems were, nor how regular were their meetings.

In general, then, pre-colonial societies in eastern Africa did not merely practice subsistence agriculture. Nonfarm activities were also in evidence, including metal working, craft industries, and the gathering of forest products. The output of these activities, and of agriculture, entered into two types of trade: sporadic periodic barter markets involving exchange within a tribe, or between neighboring tribes; and long-distance inter-tribal trade focused on the Arab-Swahili port cities of the coast. The latter was a fore-runner of the trading system that developed in the colonial era.

---

8 . W.A. Chanler, *Through Jungle and Desert: Travels in East Africa* (London: Macmillan, 1896) pp. 189-190, 343, quoted in F.E. Bernard, op. cit., p. 268.

9 . F.E. Bernard, op. cit., p. 268.

10 . See Leslie J. Wood, "The Functional Structure of a Rural Market System," *Geografiska Annaler* 57, series B (1975), p. 110.

11 . D.R. Fraser Taylor *The Role of the Smaller Urban Place in Development: A Case Study from Kenya* (Ottawa: Department of Geography and School of International Affairs, Carleton University, undated). Mimeographed.

Incipient Nonfarm Sector Activities in the Colonial Period

The construction by the British of the East African Railway from Mombasa on the Indian Ocean coast to Port Florence (Kisumu) on Lake Victoria signaled wholesale economic as well as socio-political changes in what was to become the colony and protectorate of Kenya. This massive colonial undertaking began in 1895, the year in which the British Foreign Office took over administration of the East African territories from the almost bankrupt Imperial British East Africa Company. While construction of the railway was for larger strategic reasons, its impact on the regional economy was profound. This impact involved: (1) the recouping of construction and operating costs through reorganization of "native" production and the introduction of European settlers, (2) the creation of an African labor force geared to the needs of an agrarian colonial economy, (3) the stimulation of commodity markets and settlements along the line of rail; and (4) the introduction of "shopkeeper" and "tradesman" classes from among the Indian workers imported originally to build the railway.

In 1905, Kenya was placed under the direct control of the Colonial Office. It was provided with a Governor, Executive, and a Legislative Council in 1906. In 1920, the area previously ruled by the Sultan of Zanzibar (and roughly coincident with the immediate hinterland of the coastal Swahili cities) was amalgamated with the colony of Kenya (that area inland which included the "Native Reserves" and the "Scheduled Areas" set aside for exclusive settlement by Europeans) to form the colony and protectorate of Kenya. The economy of the Reserves, however, with their mainly subsistence farmers as well as petty craftsmen and traders was not developed nor, indeed, structured so as to provide a surplus that could generate earnings capable of repaying the costs of railway construction. Consequently, the focus of commercial farm and nonfarm production moved from the Reserves to the European Scheduled Areas with their large farms and plantations.

Production in the European areas, however, could not have been organized on a sufficient scale unless African labor was available in large quantities and for minimal wages. Since Africans were initially reluctant to abandon their traditional system and work for low wages, the Government, mainly in response to settler pressures, introduced coercive measures such as hut and poll taxes levied on Africans in the Reserves. The necessity of paying these taxes forced Africans to work for extended periods outside the reserves on European farms. In 1936, these taxes were Shs20 per head for Masai

and Shs12 for other tribes. About the same time, the standard wage
for African labor on European farms was between Shs8 and Shs10 per
month. Large numbers of able bodied Africans were therefore obliged
to work to pay the poll taxes for aged and invalided kinfolk and for
widows or others who could not leave the reserves to work for white
men's wages. To prevent Africans farming as tenants in the
Scheduled Areas, the *Resident Native Ordinance* was passed by the
Legislative Council, making it a criminal offence for a native to be
the tenant of a white farmer unless the African worked for the
European for a period of not less than 180 days per annum.[12] The
limits on the length of time an individual African was permitted to
remain in the Scheduled Areas, the obligations of the migrant
laborers toward their own families or enfeebled kinfolk, and the
need to purchase their own supplies while working as laborers on
white farms (or have the costs of upkeep deducted from their minimal
wages by their employer) meant that there was little surplus
purchasing power available to the African worker after poll taxes
had been paid and other commitments had been met. This is probably
what the colonial government intended in order to keep the labor
system in operation. Still, it is probable that some cash surplus
was saved by many returning Africans, and both investments and
consumer purchases by these Africans helped establish African and
Asian enterprises in and around the Reserves. African businesses
were almost entirely dependent on the savings of the Africans
themselves until the 1950s, because there were legal restrictions on
cash loans to Africans, the maximum amounting to fifty pounds
sterling per head. Also, would-be Kenyan retailers could not buy
inventory at wholesale prices as a general rule, due to their
inadequate operating capital and to strong resistance from the
mainly Asian wholesalers against any encroachment of Africans into
trading.[13]

The Role of Asians

Apart from the residual trading functions left over from
pre-colonial days in the Bantu regions of Kenya and the effects of
wage labor on African small enterprises, the more organized and
formal part of the nonfarm sector during the colonial period in
Kenya was the preserve mainly of the Asians--immigrants and their
descendants who came from the Indian sub-continent. Actually,

---

12 . George Padmore, *How Britain Rules Africa* (New York: Lothrop, Lee and
Shepherd, 1936), pp. 120-121.

13 . Colin Leys, *Underdevelopment in Kenya: The Political Economy of
Neo-Colonialism* (London: Heinemann, 1975), p. 52.

Asians, Arabs, and Somalis had begun trading in East Africa before
the colonial period, pushing far into the interior--there is a
record of an Asian trader established at remote Lake Baringo in the
Rift Valley as early as 1885.[14] Commercial and manufacturing
occupations were about the only viable options for Indians who
remained in East Africa, since the British forbade the purchase of
agricultural land by Asians during the colonial period.
Consequently, the Indians or Asians became townsmen: the ubiquitous
dukawallahs, or petty shopkeepers, as well as tradesmen, clerks, and
urban service workers.

Unlike Africans, Indians did not endure tight restrictions on
sources of capital for investment in nonfarm activities. They came
from an economic tradition in which capital accumulation, profit
seeking, entrepreneurship, and acquisitiveness were well-established
principles. They had, moreover, been participants in the wage labor
involved in railroad construction and in government clerical
positions, which gave them the opportunity to save and invest. In
addition, according to Balachandran,[15] branches of Indian banks such
as the Bank of Baroda and Bank of India that established themselves
in East Africa were crucial in the movement of East African Asians
into larger-scale enterprises, initially trading and later
manufacturing. Indeed, up to 1921, the currency in circulation in
East Africa was based on the Indian rupee and pice (later modified
to rupees and cents, then florins and cents, and finally to
shillings and cents as at present).

Over the years, Asians gained a reputation as resourceful
traders. The first commercial dealings by Africans in and around
the African Reserves, thus, were probably with the local Asian
dukawallah or "fundi" (tradesman). These Asians, who lived in
small, remote clusters of rural *dukas* (shops) or in larger towns,
were obliged to deal competitively and to utilize every possible
advantage at their disposal to eke out a living. In some regions,
Asians came into direct competition with Africans who had entered
the arena of rural enterprise. For instance, in the Kamba areas
around Machakos, the inroads of Indian merchants and traders were
strenuously resisted by the Kamba themselves, who had retained some
of their former expertise as long distance traders even though the
peak of their trading activity had long since passed. One Kamba
elder, in response to an official's offer to bring in Asian

---

14. S. Pandit, ed., *Asians in East and Central Africa* (Nairobi: Panco
Publications, 1963), pp. 48-57.

15. P.K. Balachandran, "An Embattled Community: Asians in East Africa
Today," *African Affairs* 80 (July, 1981): 318.

shopkeepers to the District, is quoted as saying: "We don't want any Indians . . . we know how to keep shops ourselves."[16]

In other, quite remote regions, however, the Asian duka cluster was an important agent of the money economy and the first introduction of Africans to the organized rural nonfarm sector. Asians appeared to recognize that trading with the Africans for cash limited their commercial scope, since African wage levels were so low that only a poor living could be had by dealing with the few "natives" who had surplus cash from their work on European farms. Instead, Asians attempted to barter with the Africans for produce that could be exported and sold for a good profit outside the region.[17] This practice did not fit well into the European settlers' or administrators' scheme for the Africans, since it subverted the system of coerced African wage labor on European farms. As Spencer notes,

> Administrators were concerned that Indian traders, as agents of development, left a great deal to be desired. On numerous occasions traders were criticized for encouraging Africans to barter, rather than to trade for money.[18]

Along the same lines there was official criticism of Asian shopkeepers in rural centers for their " . . . Inability . . . to stock an ever-widening range of imported goods to meet the growing sophistication of the cultivators. The *dukawallahs* appeared to be conservative, unwilling to stock new lines which might give fresh impetus to Africans to produce more."[19] In their trade dealings with Africans they were accused by administrators of ignoring quality in favor of quantity, thereby reducing the value and earning potential of regional exports.[20]

It must be pointed out in this connection that African farmers were prohibited by law from cultivating specific types of cash crops such as coffee and tea which would have given them a high financial return but would have put them in direct competition with the European settlers. This prohibition on cash crop cultivation must have greatly reduced the African demand for products of the Asian-controlled rural nonfarm sector. This restriction of African demand had an adverse effect during the great depression of the 1930s, when the export market for Kenyan cash crops declined. The local economy could not be induced to take up some of the slack, due

---

16 . J. Lamphear, op. cit., p. 101.

17 . F.E. Bernard, op. cit., p. 272.

18 . I.G.R. Spencer, "The First Assault on Indian Ascendancy: Indian Traders in the Kenya Reserves 1895-1929," *African Affairs* 80 (July 1981): 331.

19 . I.G.R. Spencer, loc. cit., p. 332.

20 . Ibid., pp. 332-333.

to the above-mentioned policies of keeping down effective peasant demand.

The Asian presence in Kenya's nonfarm sector peaked during the 1960s. In 1961, over 67 percent of all locally-owned enterprises with fifty or more employees were Asian owned.[21] Most Asians were engaged in construction, trading, and repairing. In 1962, manufacturing comprised only 15 percent of the assets of Asians,[22] indicating the extent to which this group controlled wholesale and retail trading, construction, and services.

Commercial Agriculture and the Nonfarm Sector

There can be no doubt that one of the most important influences contributing to the expansion of the rural nonfarm sector was the growth of African commercial and semi-commercial agriculture in the late colonial and post-colonial periods. Major changes in African agriculture began after the Second World War, as population pressures in the Reserves mounted, urban populations grew, and the needs of the government to find sources of food and of revenue-earning exports mounted commensurately.

Pressures toward commercialization of African agriculture were exacerbated during the Mau Mau uprising of the 1950s. The proximate cause of these pressures was overcrowding in the Kikuyu Reserve in Central Province,[23] but it was clear in any case that settler-inspired controls on commercial crop production by Africans could be sustained no longer. The government commissioned a report (the Swynnerton Plan)[24] which became the basis of a new policy for African agriculture. Most students of Kenyan development acknowledge that this was a landmark in Kenya's history.[25]

The principal objective of the Swynnerton Plan was " . . . so to accelerate cash crop growing by Africans that in many cases, e.g., coffee, pyrethrum, new production will greatly exceed the present production of the established industries . . . (and will) . . . provide employment for Kikuyu repatriates both in the Reserves and on development projects, having as their main objective the raising of the agricultural productivity and the human and stock

---

21 . Colin Leys, op. cit., p. 45.

22 . P.K. Balachandran, loc. cit., p. 321.

23 . See M.P. K. Sorrenson, *Land Reform in the Kikuyu Country* (Nairobi: Oxford University Press, 1967).

24 . Colony and Protectorate of Kenya, *A Plan to Intesify the Development of African Agriculture in Kenya* (Nairobi: The Government Printer, 1954).

25 . Judith Heyer, "Agricultural Development Policy in Kenya from the Colonial Period to 1975," in *Rural Development in Tropical Africa,* ed. J. Heyer, P. Robers, and G. Williams (London: Macmillan, 1981), p. 101.

carrying capacity of the land."[26] But, as far as the rural nonfarm
sector is concerned, the most important result of the Plan was that
African smallholders began to receive cash for the sale of tea,
coffee, pyrethrum, sugar, and maize grown on their holdings and to
spend some of this cash in the duka clusters and periodic
marketplaces adjacent to the Reserve. This augmented the earnings
and remittances of Africans employed on white settler farms and in
towns. Other important effects were the establishment of
semi-governmental marketing boards which introduced agroprocessing
into smallholder rural areas (tea and coffee factories, for
example). This led more rural residents into the money economy as
laborers in processing plants. The overall success of this Plan can
be seen in the rapid expansion of cash cropping: between 1954 and
1972 the total Gross Farm Revenue originating in the small farm
sector rose from K 9.9m to K 54.8m.[27] It would be safe to assume
that a considerable proportion of this cash increase circulated
through the rural markets and towns with their growing nonfarm
enterprises.

The effects of commercialization on small-scale agriculture
were not felt equally in all parts of Kenya but were greatest in
areas with high ecological potential and a cultural history which
emphasized intensive crop cultivation (figure 2.1). Even within the
high-potential areas, increases in small-holder cash earnings were
variable, with the coffee and tea growing areas achieving the
highest growth rates up to 1972.[28] These were "creditworthy" crops,
so that farmers cultivating them were perhaps more likely to qualify
for loans from banks in the post-Independence period, and such
farmers were often in a position, consequently, to venture into
ownership of nonfarm enterprises.[29]

As Heyer points out, however, the rapid increase in small-farm
cash output until the 1970s was exceptional and probably cannot be
repeated in future.[30] This is because of internationally-set
controls on production of certain export crops like coffee and sugar
and partly because of government-imposed pricing controls set to
keep urban food and raw material inputs at acceptable price levels

---

26 . Colony and Protectorate of Kenya, op. cit., p. 59.

27 . J. Tait Davis, "Development of the Small-Farm Sector in Kenya,
1964-1972," *The Canadian Geographer* 21 (1977): 40.

28 . Ibid., p. 53.

29 . See G.N. Kitching, *Social and Economic Inequality in Rural East Africa:
The Present as a Clue to the Past* (Swansea: University College of Swansea, Centre
for Development Studies, Occasional Paper Series, 1977).

30 . Judith Heyer, op. cit., p. 117.

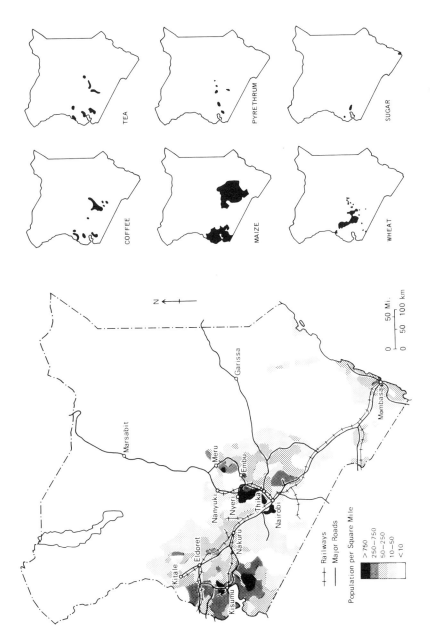

Fig. 2.1 Kenya: Patterns of population concentration and cash crop production

(given that urban areas are now centers of considerable political influence). This is likely to mean that future growth of those parts of the rural nonfarm sector that rely directly on the purchasing power of the peasant farmer may also be curtailed. This relationship will be discussed further in a later section.

The Growth of Rural Trading Centers in the Colonial Period

Many of the open-air market places that predate the colonial period attracted clusters of Asian, Swahili, or African dukas during the colonial era. Many others, however, were artifacts of colonialism and of the wish of the administration to impose a degree of spatial order on the marketing patterns of the colony. But while rural trading and craft enterprises proliferated in many areas during the colonial era, it would be a mistake to assume that colonialism had this effect in all regions. For instance, Bernard claims that in Meru District, an attitude of benign neglect on the part of the administration actually led to a diminishing of trade in the early colonial period.[31]

A word about the use of the term "periodic" in reference to African markets is in order here, since this term is employed very inconsistently in the literature. In this study, the term is taken to cover all markets and fairs which do not operate at the same level of activity daily and are not composed predominantly of permanent enterprises. A significant number of part-time or mobile enterprises are found in these markets. The term "periodic market" is thus used here to signify a market in which some permanent enterprises exist but which also expands on certain "special market days" due to a regular influx of part-time and mobile entrepreneurs and their rural clintele.[32] We reserve the term "purely periodic" for those markets which are deserted at other times than market days.

The Internal Organization of Rural Markets

As the specific environment in which many (and perhaps most) nonfarm enterprises operate, marketplaces in East Africa tend to have numerous characteristics in common. Most have at least some permanent structures, usually "dukas" or stores occupied by the retailers and their families who live on the premises. Some smaller, purely periodic centers exist, but this type is less common

---

31. Frank E. Bernard, op. cit., p. 117.

32. For an overview of the literature on periodic marketing see R.J. Bromley, *Periodic Markets, Daily Markets and Fairs: A Bibliography* (Swansea: University College of Swansea, Centre for Development Studies, Occasional Papers, 1977)

than it used to be. In most cases, whether through the efforts of
administrators, the local county councils, or through church or
other influences, there is a recognizable order in the internal
layout of the centers. Verification of this comes from previous
researchers as well as from the observations of the present authors.

The permanent duka structures usually face a market square or
road, often set back some distance from the vehicular thoroughfare.
Older ones are often constructed of adobe or mud and wattle, with
corrugated iron roofs. More modern dukas may be constructed of
concrete blocks or stucco. Pillared awnings covered with corrugated
iron roofing usually protect the fronts of the dukas from rain and
sun. Often, the entire front of the duka may be opened up to give
adequate air circulation and customer access, with heavy wooden
shutters or wrought iron screens giving security when the duka is
closed after business hours. On market days, space under these
awnings or doorways may be sub-let by tailors, seamstresses, or
other entrepreneurs. Interspersed among the permanent dukas may be
other buildings used for special purposes on market days or other
occasions, for example, butcheries, garages, bars or restaurants,
and rudimentary wooden stalls or shelters.

Even in the "open air" parts of these market centers, there is
often considerable spatial regularity. For example, the sellers of
particular types of commodities will often cluster together in a
customary part of the market square, where buyers will easily be
able to locate them and compare wares and prices. Manufacturing,
cattle sales, transportation depots, and services will also be found
in designated parts of the open market.

Examples of some fairly typical market center layouts, based
on observations from the 1977 Central Province Survey, are given in
figure 2.2. Other examples of market center layouts are described
by Charles Good, dealing with Ankole in Uganda; Reinhardt Henkel,
covering parts of Western Kenya; and Robert Obudho, dealing with
classes of rural centers in Kenya.[33]

Planned and Unplanned Colonial Market Systems
The colonial government organized a system of three functional
classes of market centers in rural Kenya. There were:

33 . See Charles M. Good, *Rural Markets and Trade in East Africa,* Research
Paper no. 128. (Chicago: University of Chicago, Department of Geography, 1970),
pp. vii-ix; and Reinhard Henkel, *Central Places in Western Kenya,* Geographic
Institute Publication no. 54 (Heidelberg: University of Heidelberg, 1979), p. 2;
R.A. Obudho, "Temporal Periodicity and Locational Spacing of Periodic and Daily
Markets in Kenya," *Cahiers d'Études Africaines* 16 (1977): 533-66.

32

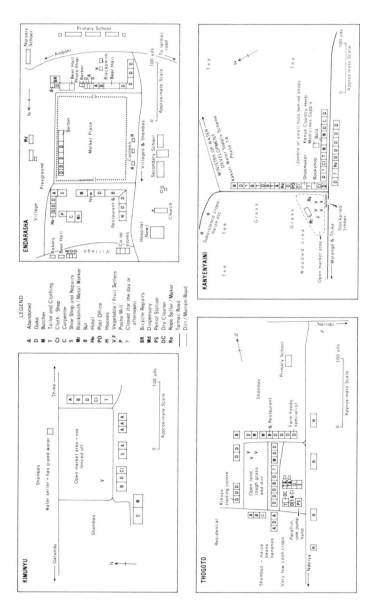

Fig. 2.2 Typical spatial forms of small Kenyan marketplaces

1. Native open barter marketplaces (these were often purely periodic, operating one or two days per week and mostly trading in foodstuffs

2. Trading centers (often located at barter marketplaces) which included some permanent dukas and which traded some manufactured goods in addition to local produce

3. Towns/retail centers/wholesale centers which traded a wider range of goods and services and which had long-distance trade linkages (here also there were permanent dukas).

As might be expected, given the necessity for Africans to pay cash taxes, markets were concentrated in areas of high agricultural output.[34] But these did not correspond with settlements in all cases. For example, many open marketplaces in the Reserves continued to lack permanent settlements, as in pre-colonial times. Also, purely dormitory settlements called labor lines sprang up in the larger European estates and plantations. In addition, there were spatial systems of settlements established by the colonial regime that were not directly connected to marketing but which served other functions. Henkel, for example, lists five locational types of centers during the colonial period:

1. Colonial administrative centers (to which social and economic activities were later added, e.g., Kapenguria in West Kenya)

2. Boundary markets (open-air, periodic, barter produce, or cattle markets)

3. Trading centers (shop centers) with clusters of Asian dukas, often at transport junctions

4. Mission stations which were, as a rule, separated from administrative centers of the colonial government

5. Traditional chief's seats, which also tended to acquire other social and economic functions.

Clearly, in some of these centers, the incipient rural nonfarm sector was growing and evolving while in other settlements there was little if any of these commercial activities.

So long as the colonial administration held supreme power over African affairs, the pattern of rural marketplaces was kept within certain bounds. The colonial administration clearly reflected the ideas of the home country as regards the "proper" pattern of rural settlements and marketplaces. Thus, Henkel quotes a British administrator as decreeing: "The layout should as far as possible approximate an English village, with the activities grouped round a

---

34. L.J. Wood, "Population Density and Rural Market Provision," *Cahiers d'Études Africaines* 14 (1974): 724.

village green, planted with good shade trees."35

In the late colonial period, there were changes in African political, social, and economic structures that had profound impacts on the whole rural nonfarm sector. First, after the Second World War, numerous African ex-servicemen returned, men who had experienced a world that gave them broader perspectives, greater expectations, and money in their pockets--their pay and gratuities, which many opted to invest in the purchase of trading plots in the rural market centers in the Reserves. For example, the District Officer in Nyeri reported in 1949 that there were 60 markets and shopping centers in the District, comprising 971 commercial plots outside of Nyeri township, serving a population of 208,000 people. This meant about one duka for every 215 people in the District, each duka being required by Government regulations to have a minimum investment of nearly 300 pounds per plot.36 A welter of regulations, however, continued to dissuade Africans from overcrowding the rural nonfarm sector and destroying the incipient system of central places the administation was trying to erect. For instance, Local Native Councils had been given the duty since the 1930s of granting trading licenses.37 But these were exclusively for the market centers then in existence, and a law stipulated that "no native shall, within a distance of three miles from the external boundaries of any market hawk, sell, barter, or expose for sale or barter any article whatsoever without express written permission of the D.C."38 In Nyanza, colonial administrators planned to add facilities such as schools, courts, police stations, and social halls to existing trading centers, and to provide properly aligned streets and electricity lines.39 There was even a plan to construct additional markets such that a system or network of trading centers 15 miles apart would develop in specific areas.40

Another factor with direct bearing on the spatial development of the rural nonfarm sector was the Emergency, occasioned by the Kikuyu rebellion which blossomed into a full-scale struggle for independence during the 1950s (as we have seen, this had an even more profound impact on African agriculture). Following their

---

35. Reinhard Henkel, op. cit., p. 229.

36. J.D. Penwill, "Report on Trades and Markets in Nyeri, 3-7 January 1949," Trade and Commerce File 6/16/11/2, Kenya National Archives, quoted in Colin Leys, op. cit., p. 51.

37. Reinhard Henkel, op. cit., p. 58.

38. Ibid., p. 227.

39. Ibid., p. 228.

40. Ibid., p. 228.

successful practice in a similar emergency in Malaya, the British
authorities forced the Kikuyu into fortified villages and
repatriated Kikuyu and others from larger towns and cities. This
forced villagization established a pattern of living which was alien
to the Kikuyu up to this point. It most certainly increased the
exposure of many Africans to the commercial economy and the
possibilities of earning an income from trading or petty
manufacturing in the small rural villages that were a legacy of the
Emergency.

The Swynnerton Plan of 1954, which changed the face of
small-scale farming, contained several provisions which also changed
the rural nonfarm sector. These were:

1. Land tenure changes, away from the communal githaka system of
   scattered plots and to consolidated, freehold, enclosed
   parcels and "duka square" sites
2. Permission to market cash crops and other farm products
   previously reserved for white farmers, notably coffee, tea
   and milk, and to expand commercial production generally
3. Access to credit primarily for farm improvements, but also
   for nonfarm enterprises), extension services to assist in
   cultivation of cash crops, and improved marketing
   infrastructures for Africans.[41]

As a result of these measures, the rural nonfarm sector acquired
many recruits from among the landless class of unsuccessful rural
residents who were not granted freehold title to an enclosed plot of
land. As we have stressed, however, the heightened agricultural
activity occasioned by land reform, and the cash income now
available to farmers, were probably the main factors stimulating
activity in the rural nonfarm sector in the late colonial period.
Similar improvements in agriculture in Uganda and Tanganyika during
this period also spurred Kenyan manufacturing and servicing
industries, with such industries heavily oriented toward
agroprocessing and farm input supply.

The Nonfarm Sector in the Post-Colonial Period

At the beginning of the Kenyatta era of independent Kenya,
therefore, there was an upsurge in peasant farming, an increasing
number of smallholders moving into cash crop production, and an
increasing number of rural Africans who were landless. Many of the
latter were obliged to follow the colonial pattern of circular

41. Colony and Protectorate of Kenya, op. cit., quoted in Arthur Hazlewood,
the Economy of Kenya: The Kenyatta Era (London: Oxford University Press, 1979), p.
10.

migration to towns or large-farm regions where they worked for a
period to earn cash to support their families. With government
encouragement, Africans were increasingly taking over from Asians as
small-scale rural businessmen, especially in petty retail trading,
transportation, social services, and some forms of small-scale
manufacturing.

These trends continued for much of the Kenyatta era, which
ended with the First President's death in 1978. This era could be
described as one in which the rural areas witnessed progressive
Africanization of cash cropping at small and medium scales and
Africanization of commerce (both of jobs and ownership) in the
market centers and towns. It also was characterized by greater
penetration of trans-national capital into manufacturing and urban
services, government involvement in marketing and servicing via the
parastatal sector, and a retreat by both Asians and Europeans into
more capital-intensive forms of production. Africans were still
largely excluded from such activities because they lacked
opportunities to acquire technical expertise and financial
resources.

The Present System of Market Centers

In rural market centers the County Councils, successors of the
Local Native Councils, took over the control of licensing traders
and other nonfarm entrepreneurs. They attempted to regulate numbers
of new operators as before, but tended to grant new licenses
exclusively to Africans, gradually squeezing the Asians out of the
smaller centers altogether. In various regions of the country,
economic functions became extremely dispersed and the numbers of
small commercial African enterprises mushroomed. For example, the
District Joint Loans Boards handed out over 8,000 small business
loans between 1965 and 1971.[42] These loans totalled K£ 1.2 million,
disbursed in small amounts of around £200-300. In addition, the
Small Loans Programme of the Industrial and Commercial Development
Corporation--a government parastatal organization--disbursed
additional loans to Africans in rural and urban areas. A key
feature of the loan recipients, however, was that they tended to be
proprietors of larger and more established enterprises, so that
these government loans did not aid those at the lower end of the
nonfarm sector. This point is explored further in later chapters.
Distribution of wholesale goods to African retailers, a source of
difficulty for small entrepreneurs during the colonial period, was

---

42. Colin Leys, op. cit., p. 151.

partially reorganized with the aid of a Government parastatal, the
Kenyan National Trading Corporation.

Central Government planners soon became alarmed at this
proliferation and dispersal of tiny rural enterprises. Trained and
advised by Western expatriates and imbued with the prevailing
doctrine that urban industrial concentration (via growth centers)
was the key to national development,[43] planners did their best to
halt the dispersal of the nonfarm sector. County councils were
urged to restrict the proliferation of small rural markets.
Instead, the intent was to foster the growth of centralized
functions in "strong growth centers."[44] The Department of Physical
Planning in the Ministry of Lands and Settlement set up a fourfold
hierarchy of centers which it envisaged would provide the needed
system of growth centers to bring about desired development. These
were: urban centers, rural centers, market centers, and local
centers.[45]

The number, distribution, and nature of market centers in
rural Kenya is therefore partly an outgrowth of set policies of the
colonial and post-colonial periods and responses to these by the
expatriate and indigenous populations. The extent to which colonial
and post-colonial governments built on pre-existing traditional
market systems is a matter of debate. However, the current market
system is in a continuous state of change and modification, under
the influence of economic, social, and political factors outlined
above. In 1974, Wood estimated that there were 984 official rural
markets (but many more unofficial ones, most probably), with
variations in market density from district to district in accordance
with population and agricultural densities.[46] Since Wood's study,
there have undoubtedly been many additions and deletions to the
market center system. Carr mentions the loss of a number of smaller
markets from the Murang'a (Central Province) market system in the
recent period.[47] The most recently available complete listing of
urban and rural centers and their populations remains that published
in the 1969 Census. Obudho[48] classifies the contemporary markets in

43. For example, see S. Kimani and D.R.F. Taylor, *Growth Centres and Rural Development* (Thika, Kenya: Maxim Printers 1973); and also Harry Richardson, "Growth Centres, Rural Development and National Urban Policy: A Defence," *International Regional Science Review* 3 (1978): 133-152.

44. Reinhard Henkel, op. cit., p. 68.

45. Republic of Kenya, *Development Plan 1974-78 Part I* (Nairobi: Government Printer, 1974), pp. 141-143.

46. L.J. Wood, op. cit., p. 717.

47. J.L. Carr, *The Function and Development of Rural Market System, Murang'a District, Kenya* (Cambridge, 1979). Mimeograph.

Kenya into daily markets and periodic markets. He further
subdivides these into:

Daily Markets	Periodic Markets
(a) covered urban markets	(a) twice weekly open air markets
(b) coastal open markets	(b) weekly open air markets
(c) rural open markets	(c) seasonal markets

Obudho goes on to discuss the functions of Kenyan markets. He
says they are places where "people meet regularly in order to
acquire and/or dispose of the locally produced and imported goods
and services, to exchange 'news' (gossip) with relatives, friends
and strangers, and to engage in recreational activities."[49]
Following Hodder, Obudho distinguishes somewhat different functions
in daily and periodic markets, noting that "periodic markets
are . . . most characteristic of food surplus areas while daily
markets are most characteristic of food deficit areas."[50]

Obudho observes that most periodic markets in Kenya have
special market days once a week, or several times per week on the
same days each time. In Central Province, among market centers
sampled in the 1977 survey by the authors, however, there was a
relatively even distribution of special market days over each day of
the week (this is discussed further in chapter 4). About 46 percent
of sampled markets were periodic in the sense of scheduling special
market days. Thirty percent of the sample had two special market
days per week (the most common pattern is Wednesday-Saturday), 12
percent had a single special market day per week, while 4 percent
had three special market days per week. Carr suggests that
bi-weekly market days reflect a pre-colonial, four day week.[51]

Obudho claims that the markets of rural Kenya are organized
into a ring system.[52] The concept of market rings is generally taken
to imply that there is a deliberate spatial and temporal
synchronization of periodic market days and locations, accommodating
movement of the mobile entrepreneurs who sell to consumers and buy
from producers in these marketplaces. However, Obudho does not
supply evidence of such movement patterns nor of the detailed
synchronous linkages among markets in specific rings. Carr states
that in Murang'a District, "linkages between markets criss-cross to

48 . R.A. Obudho, op. cit., p. 556.
49 . Ibid., p. 558.
50 . Ibid., p. 556.
51 . J.L. Carr, op. cit., pp. 8-9.
52 . R.A. Obudho, op. cit., p. 561.

such an extent that market cycles are unrecognizable."[53] Freeman, in
a study of mobile entrepreneurs in Central Province, found that
movement patterns did not approximate rings but were much less
regular or sophisticated. They appeared more as a commuting pattern
from a home base to linearly arranged markets, this movement pattern
being termed a "market shuttle."[54]

The system of enterprise regulation in the Kenyatta era, based
on *The Trade Licencing Act of 1968,* and the drive to plan market
systems was thus only partially successful in halting the
unstructured growth of the rural nonfarm sector. Some businesses
simply operated without licenses and hence outside the law--for
instance the *matatu* taxis and workshops of the urban slums, and
family handicraft enterprises operated on remote farmsteads and in
the bush. In the eyes of the government, however, even the smallest
activity, the meanest hawker, required a license. Harassment of
illegal traders and craftsmen by police was a feature in the
marketplaces, slums, and roadsides of Kenya. In the end, the
government appears to have acknowledged that its efforts to sandbag
the dykes of regulated trade to prevent the flood of small illegal
enterprises has not succeeded. For example, harassment of matatu
taxi operators was officially halted some years ago. This was in
keeping with the pragmatism of the late Kenyatta era, which some
have characterized as a blend of laissez faire capitalism and
African socialism.[55]

Future Trends

In the first years of the Moi era, the rural nonfarm sector
has achieved a measure of government recognition as a potential tool
in rural development and has been recognized formally in the
recently completed Development Plan (1979-83). Africanization of
the sector is far advanced. The government has stepped up its
program of construction of farm to market roads which is aiding the
expansion of the rural nonfarm sector in the villages and periodic
marketplaces. Relaxation of controls on the operation of matatu
taxis, which appear as the most efficient form of rural
transportation over much of Kenya, has clearly helped the expansion
of this sector. Unfortunately, the tightening of other restrictions
by the government, such as the prohibition of imports of used

---

53. J.L. Carr, op. cit., p. 18.

54. Donald B. Freeman, "Mobile Enterprises and Markets in Central Province,
Kenya," *Geographical Review* 70 (1980): 45.

55. World Bank, *Kenya: Into the Second Decade* (Baltimore: Johns Hopkins
University Press for the World Bank, 1975), p. 4.

clothing, have had an adverse effect on some parts of the sector.
Manufacturing as well as trading, on the whole, have held their own
in rural areas against the inroads of imported manufactures in
certain products and service lines at least. It is necessary at
this point to discuss the structure of the contemporary nonfarm
sector to establish the extent to which the sector has preserved its
economic health. This will form the subject of the following
chapter.

CHAPTER III

THE NATURE AND STRUCTURE OF THE RURAL NONFARM SECTOR IN KENYA: NATIONAL AND REGIONAL PATTERNS

In the previous chapter the historical evolution of the rural nonfarm sector was shown to fall into three quite distinct phases that reflect the flow and ebb of the British colonial tide: the pre-colonial reciprocity and barter trading phase, the colonial period when many Indian traders and artisans established a nationwide system of trading and petty commodity production, and the present post-colonial phase in which the nonfarm sector has undergone progressive Africanization. In this chapter we describe the outcome of these historical processes. We examine, in turn, the present structure and geographical distribution of the rural nonfarm sector at the national, provincial, and local levels.

While we emphasize the *supply* of nonfarm products and jobs that are an outgrowth of historical developments, we must first examine another facet of the colonial legacy, one that conditions and (to some extent) accounts for particular structural characteristics of the rural nonfarm sector. This is the factor of *demand* for nonfarm goods and services in contemporary Kenya. Of greatest significance is rural demand for these products, which displays important regional variations in nature and influence.

Rural Demand for Goods and Services

Purchases of goods and services by Kenyan rural households, whether through cash transactions or barter, account for a substantial proportion of household expenditure and, moreover, have been growing year by year. It has been estimated that, in the mid-nineteen seventies, the average rural household spent K £ 108 per year, of which K £ 65 (or 60 percent) was spent on food, K £16 on clothing, and K £ 3.25 on appliances, utensils, and furnishings.[1] Even rural households with less than 1 hectare spent K £ 83 per year, of which K £ 56 was spent on food and K £ 10 on clothing. These data

---

1. Arthur Hazlewood, *The Economy of Kenya: The Kenyatta Era* (London: Oxford University Press, 1979), p. 83.

41

indicate that the very smallest farms and poorest peasant households either manage to generate some cash surplus, engage in off-farm work for cash, or receive cash remittances that enable them to buy necessities.[2]

Some general observations on the pattern of aggregate rural demand for nonfarm sector produce need to be made. The rising demand for these products and services results partly from rising real incomes amongst some segments of the rural population, but more fundamentally it is due to the rapid increase in rural population.

Sources of Rural Household Needs

Where do rural households in Kenya obtain their basic needs? The evidence reveals five possible sources for needs like food, clothing, shoes, pots and pans, and beds and tables: they may be produced within the farmer's own holding (subsistence production); they may be produced by neighboring households (barter or cash exchanges); they may be purchased in local "dukas" or stores, or in market centers (either periodic or permanent); or, finally, they may be purchased in towns, often in "formal" larger-scale enterprises. The pattern of purchases by rural households amongst these five sources was the subject of an IRS nonfarm survey module conducted in 1977-78. The results of this survey are revealed in figure 3.1.[3]

The results indicate that, at the national level, Kenyan consumers appear to behave in a fashion similar to their Western counterparts as regards market travel and purchasing patterns. That is, they are unwilling to travel long distances for items frequently consumed and for which comparison shopping is not necessary but will travel longer distances for major items that are purchased infrequently, such as furniture. Thus, food, a basic daily need, is obtained mostly from "home grown" produce on a farmer's own holding, reflecting the predominantly subsistence nature of Kenyan rural life (figure 3.1A). But nearly 29 percent of households obtain their food needs primarily from rural market centers, where farm produce vendors tend to congregate on special market days. At the other extreme, 45 percent of rural households purchase their household furnishing (beds and tables) in a larger town, which in Kenya would involve the average rural resident in a fairly long journey to shop for the needed items.

---

2. Republic of Kenya, Central Bureau of Statistics, *Integrated Rural Survey 1974-75* (Nairobi: Government Printer, 1977), table 8.8, p. 56.

3. Based on figure 3 (p. 34) in D.B. Freeman and G.B. Norcliffe, "The Rural Nonfarm Sector: Development Opportunity or Employer of Last Resort?" *Ceres: The F.A.O. Review on Agriculture and Development* 16 (January-February 1983): pp. 28-34.

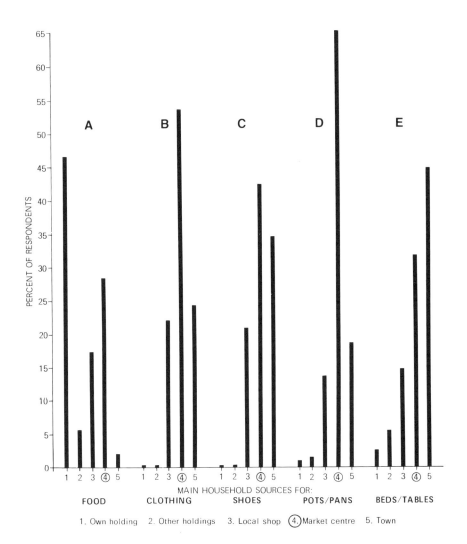

Fig. 3.1 Sources of household needs in rural Kenya

The most important aspect of the rural purchasing pattern shown in figure 3.1 is the predominance of rural market centers as sources of household goods in all cases except for the purchase of food and furniture. Proportions of households listing market centers as the main source of purchases is greatest for kitchen utensils (pots/pans) where more than 65 percent of respondents shopped at market centers, and for clothing, where the proportion was almost 57 percent of households. For these items, other possible sources (farm holdings, local "dukas", and towns) were less than half as important.

A number of factors help explain the significance of rural market centers. First, as noted earlier, these small market places are closely spaced throughout the high-potential agricultural areas of Kenya. They are periodic in the sense that, although they usually have permanent dukas, they exhibit increased activity on several days (special market days) per week as a rule. They thus give peasants an opportunity to purchase frequently needed items as well as occasionally-acquired comparison goods without having to travel long distances. This means farmers or their families are not obliged to spend excessive amounts of time away from the task of cultivating crops, nor do they incur high travel costs. The same advantages obtain for those who are part-time vendors of nonfarm products but who also have a smallholding. In markets which have a periodic component, entrepreneurs who sell "high order" goods are able to reach a demand threshold that makes their activities economically viable. Given the relatively low average purchasing power of the Kenyan rural population, they would not be viable if located every day in the same place.

Haggling to reach an agreed price between buyer and seller is a feature of these markets. Requests for credit by indigent consumers are, however, less frequent among the small, part-time or mobile enterprises than in the case of the local permanent dukas.

These features of the small rural market centers in Kenya are advantageous to rural consumers and "penny capitalist" entrepreneurs alike and undoubtedly help to account for the existence of a periodic component in Kenyan markets. They also explain the increasing numbers of rural nonfarm enterprises frequenting these centers.

Regional Patterns of Demand for Nonfarm Sector Products

While the predominance of market centers noted in the national level pattern is encountered throughout most regions of Kenya, there

are some significant regional differences in consumer purchasing
patterns for various household needs. These are shown in tables 3.1
to 3.5. Regional patterns of purchasing for five major items--food,
clothing, shoes, kitchen utensils, and furniture--are discussed in
turn.

Food

Table 3.1 shows which provinces of Kenya are still most
dependent on subsistence sources and which have mostly fully adopted
an exchange economy. Rift Valley, Western, and Nyanza provinces,
all relatively remote from the urban "hub" of Kenya, are most
reliant on subsistence food production. Provinces closer to the
Nairobi-Mombasa corridor, namely Central, Eastern, and Coast
provinces, are less reliant on subsistence production, but more
dependent on purchases from the nearest food source, usually the
local duka or market center. In Coast Province, over half of the
sampled rural households shopped most frequently for food at the
local duka (table 3.1). Towns were an insignificant source of
household food purchases, involving less than 5 percent in nearly
all provinces. In Eastern Province, much of which does not have
high agricultural potential, reliance on market centers for food
purchases reaches more than 40 percent, as is also the case in
Nyanza Province.

Clothing

As one might expect in a country that has moved some distance
away from a full subsistence economy, very few households in the
surveyed areas make their own clothes. Most households purchase
such items from dukas or market vendors. In all Kenyan provinces
except Coast and Nyanza, market centers are the principal source of
clothing (table 3.2). In Nyanza and Coast provinces, in contrast,
clothing purchases are fairly evenly distributed amongst local
dukas, market centers, and towns. It should be noted that, at the
time of the survey, much of the clothing purchased from market
centers was used clothing, imported duty-free from Europe and North
America. Subsequently such imports have been banned as a result of
lobbying by the domestic textile industry. In Coast Province and
pastoral areas of Rift Valley and Eastern provinces, more
traditional forms of clothing are worn, and in these areas, used
Western-style clothing is less in evidence in dukas and market
stalls. This difference in clothing styles and the associated
reliance in certain areas on used clothing help explain
interprovincial differences in the pattern of household purchases of
clothing.

46

TABLE 3.1

MAIN SOURCE OF HOUSEHOLD NEEDS BY PROVINCE (PERCENT)

FOOD

Province*	No. of Responses	Where obtained				
		Own Holding	Other Holdings	Local Duka	Market Center	Town
Central	289	32.9	3.8	41.5	21.8	0.0
Rift Valley	391	65.0	10.5	5.6	14.6	4.3
Western	279	64.1	5.0	2.1	28.7	0.0
Nyanza	455	50.3	2.6	3.1	42.8	1.1
Eastern	474	39.2	5.5	13.3	40.7	1.3
Coast	267	25.1	4.5	55.8	9.4	5.2
National Level	2,155	46.9	5.4	17.3	28.4	1.9

SOURCE: IRS Nonfarm Module 2, 1977-78. (Unpublished.)

NOTE: Row totals may not add exactly to 100% due to rounding.

*Nairobi and Northeastern provinces excluded from survey.

TABLE 3.2

MAIN SOURCE OF HOUSEHOLD NEEDS BY PROVINCE (PERCENT)

CLOTHING

Province*	No. of Responses	Where obtained				
		Own Holding	Other Holdings	Local Duka	Market Center	Town
Central	289	0.3	0.3	13.8	78.9	6.6
Rift Valley	391	0.0	0.0	20.7	51.2	28.1
Western	279	0.0	0.0	13.6	69.5	16.8
Nyanza	455	0.6	0.2	38.7	36.7	23.7
Eastern	474	0.0	0.2	7.8	62.6	29.3
Coast	267	0.4	1.1	36.3	25.1	37.1
National Level	2,155	0.2	0.3	21.8	53.5	24.2

SOURCE: IRS Nonfarm Module 2, 1977-78. (Unpublished.)

NOTE: Includes secondhand clothing; row totals may not add to 100% due to rounding.

*Nairobi and Northeastern provinces excluded from survey.

Shoes

In many rural areas of Kenya, Western-style manufactured shoes are uncommon among the adult and juvenile population. The proportion of households in which shoes are never, or rarely, purchased is highest in Coast and Eastern provinces. Very few households make or sell shoes to other rural residents (table 3.3). Market centers are the main source of shoes for at least forty percent of households in Central, Rift Valley, Eastern and Western provinces, while towns are the principal sources for more than forty percent of households in Rift Valley, Western, and Coast provinces. Only in Nyanza Province do more than forty percent of householders purchase shoes at a local "duka." Unlike clothing, there is not a large market for second hand shoes in Kenya. Sandals made out of pieces of used leather or worn automobile tires are, however, common in some parts of the country.

TABLE 3.3

MAIN SOURCE OF HOUSEHOLD NEEDS BY PROVINCE (PERCENT)

SHOES

| Province* | No. of Responses | Where obtained | | | | |
		Own Holding	Other Holdings	Local Duka	Market Center	Town
Central	289	0.7	0.3	24.2	59.2	15.6
Rift Valley	391	0.0 (0.0)**	0.0	10.5	47.3	42.2
Western	279	0.0 (0.7)**	0.0	16.1	42.0	41.2
Nyanza	455	0.4 (0.9)**	0.2	42.8	24.2	31.4
Eastern	474	0.2 (1.7)**	0.2	7.4	59.9	30.6
Coast	267	0.0 (8.6)**	0.4	23.6	15.0	52.4
National Level	2,155	0.2 (1.7)**	0.2	20.8	42.1	34.9

SOURCE: IRS Nonfarm Module 2, 1977-78. (Unpublished.)

NOTE: Row totals do not necessarily add to 100% due to rounding.

* Nairobi and Northeastern provinces omitted from survey.

** Percent who do not wear shoes.

Kitchen Utensils (Pots and Pans)

Most rural householders purchase kitchen utensils in market centers. In fact, in Western, Nyanza, and Eastern provinces, more than seventy percent of sampled households listed market centers as the main source of these items (table 3.4). Rural holdings themselves produce and sell negligible amounts of this household need, while local dukas are only of minor importance. Purchases in towns are only important in two provinces: Rift Valley (31 percent of households), and Coast Province (43 percent of households). As in the case of used clothing, kitchen utensils lend themselves to exchange in open market places, since small-scale, travelling traders can carry them easily from one market to the next in matatu taxis, simply by "nesting" smaller utensils inside larger ones,

TABLE 3.4

MAIN SOURCE OF HOUSEHOLD NEEDS BY PROVINCE (PERCENT)

POTS/PANS

Province[*]	No. of Responses	Where obtained				
		Own Holding	Other Holdings	Local Duka	Market Center	Town
Central	289	0.1 (0.0)[**]	0.0	24.2	56.1	18.7
Rift Valley	391	0.0 (0.0)[**]	0.0	12.5	56.5	30.9
Western	279	0.4 (0.0)[**]	0.0	4.6	92.1	3.0
Nyanza	456	0.4 (0.4)[**]	3.5	19.3	72.6	3.7
Eastern	374	0.3 (0.0)[**]	1.6	8.6	70.8	18.7
Coast	267	3.0 (0.7)[**]	2.0	13.1	38.2	42.7
National Level	2,056	0.7 (0.2)[**]	1.4	13.9	65.1	18.7

SOURCE: IRS Nonfarm Module 2, 1977-78. (Unpublished.)

NOTE: Row totals may not add exactly to 100% due to rounding.

[*] Nairobi and Northeastern provinces excluded from survey.

[**] Percent who do not use these items.

making them more portable and resistant to damage in transport.4 Although less frequently demanded than perishable produce, utensils have a high enough per-unit price that an adequate return can be had by a small vendor even under highly competitive conditions, provided the vendor is prepared to travel to a sufficient number of periodic markets each week.

Furniture (Beds and Tables)

Furniture is the one item among the household needs investigated in the CBS survey in which purchases in towns generally predominate over purchases in rural marketplaces. Only in Central and Wes.ern provinces are marketplaces listed as the main source by a majority of households (table 3.5). Clearly, items such as beds and tables are not the types of goods that could be easily transported by mobile entrepreneurs among periodic marketplaces. They are, moreover, not frequently purchased by the average household. They are thus items that, as in Western central places, are generally found in permanent shops or workshops in larger centers that draw customers from a wide hinterland.

Effects of Regional Demand Patterns

Regional variations in the demand for nonfarm products directly influence the distribution and organization of nonfarm activities. The price of goods and the frequency of repeat purchases affect the place where a commodity will be traded. The ability of vendors to remain viable despite minimal capitalization and vigorous competition is also a factor. In some cases, for example where high unit price or low turn-over rates of goods are involved, demand conditions virtually dictate that such goods must be sold from permanent dukas in larger towns. But in a significant minority of instances, competitive conditions permit small, mobile vendors or craftsmen to make and/or sell the items in open periodic

---

4. D.B. Freeman, "Mobile Enterprises and Markets in Central Province, Kenya," *Geographical Review* 70 (1980): 36-49.

TABLE 3.5

MAIN SOURCE OF HOUSEHOLD NEEDS BY PROVINCE (PERCENT)

BEDS/TABLES

Province[*]	No. of Responses	Where obtained				
		Own Holding	Other Holdings	Local Duka	Market Center	Town
Central	289	0.7 ** (0.0)	0.3	22.1	54.3	22.5
Rift Valley	383	0.0 ** (0.0)	0.3	6.3	31.1	62.4
Western	279	0.0 ** (0.0)	0.0	15.1	43.7	41.2
Nyanza	455	2.2 ** (1.8)	2.8	29.7	24.4	39.1
Eastern	474	5.9 ** (0.2)	9.5	3.4	30.4	50.6
Coast	267	5.2 ** (1.5)	22.1	13.1	11.6	46.4
National Level	2,147	2.5 ** (0.6)	5.5	14.7	31.9	44.8

SOURCE: IRS Nonfarm Module 2, 1977-78. (Unpublished.)

NOTE: Row totals may not add exactly to 100% due to rounding.

[*] Nairobi and Northeastern provinces excluded from survey.

[**] Households never using these items.

marketplaces and yet earn an adequate living. The fact that many vendors are also farmers (or families of farmers) has an added effect, reducing vendor mobility and the frequency with which they will participate in the marketplace. This possibly helps to condition the pattern of market periodicity.[5] Spatial factors such as distance from Nairobi, the density of rural population, the

---

5. D.B. Freeman, op. cit.

distribution of high-potential cropland, the incidence of commercial as opposed to subsistence production, and attitudes to Western lifestyles as against traditional customs all play a part in bringing about the regional variation in demand outlined above. These, in turn, condition the patterns of nonfarm sector activity in rural Kenya and help explain its structure, which will be discussed in detail below.

The Structure of the Rural Nonfarm Sector

The rural nonfarm sector can be subdivided into two types of activity. The first comprises dispersed activities, which are usually carried on as adjuncts to agriculture in rural farmsteads. The second is conducted in market centers and tends more toward organization on a full-time basis in small-scale enterprises that specialize in one or a few products or services. The latter operate either in permanent locations, or in the guise of mobile enterprises. The dividing line between the dispersed and market types of nonfarm activity is often blurred, especially in the case of part-time or seasonal participation by farm families.

We will begin by describing some of the general characteristics of the nonfarm sector, before turning to a more detailed discussion of specific activities and regional patterns in nonfarm enterprises. The data for this general overview of the nonfarm sector are drawn from two nonfarm modules conducted as part of the Integrated Rural Survey by the Kenyan Central Bureau of Statistics in 1977-78. This survey sampled small farm areas in all provinces except Northeastern and Nairobi provinces. Details of this and other surveys are given in the Appendix.

The first nonfarm module sampled 2,232 households, in each of which two simple questions were asked: (1) Has any income-earning nonfarm activity been carried on in this household for a month or more in the year prior to the survey? (2) If so, name the activity or activities. Two important results of this frequency count are contained in tables 3.6 and 3.7. Table 3.6 shows that nonfarm activities are indeed very prevalent in rural households throughout Kenya and are a major contributor to rural incomes. In fact, 51 percent of all households in the national sample practiced some form of nonfarm activity. Almost a quarter of all households carried on two or more activities during the same period, indicating a significant division of effort between farming and nonfarm employment in such households. Over two percent of sampled households recorded more than five distinctly different activities.

TABLE 3.6

THE PREVALENCE OF NONFARM ACTIVITIES IN RURAL HOUSEHOLDS OF KENYA: A COMPARISON OF
PROVINCIAL AND NATIONAL DATA

Frequency of Nonfarm Activities per Sample Household	Central %*	Coast %*	Eastern %*	Nyanza %*	Rift Valley %*	Western %*	National Level %*
0	63.8	31.4	49.9	39.4	58.8	44.3	49.6
1	24.7	48.4	26.3	23.5	20.3	32.8	26.4
2	9.0	12.1	11.2	20.0	11.2	11.8	13.0
3	1.4	5.6	3.6	7.4	5.9	4.0	4.7
4	0.6	2.4	2.5	3.5	2.5	3.1	2.5
5	0.6	--	1.5	2.9	0.2	1.5	1.3
Over 5	--	--	5.0	3.3	1.1	2.5	2.4
Total Sample	100.0	100.0	100.0	100.0	100.0	100.0	100.0
Average no. of Activities/H'hold	0.52	0.99	1.07	1.34	0.78	1.03	.97
Households in Sample	354	126	475	515	439	323	2232

SOURCE: IRS Nonfarm Module 1, 1977.

NOTE: Percentage figures may not add exactly to 100 due to rounding.

*Percentage of Provincial Samples

The incidence of nonfarm activities in rural households at the provincial level is also given in table 3.6. Clear differences are evident in the pattern of activity from province to province. Nyanza and Coast provinces record around two-thirds of their sample households with some nonfarm activities, which is appreciably above the national average. In contrast, Central Province and Rift Valley Province have considerably lower frequencies of nonfarm occupations per household. Nyanza and Eastern provinces are notable for the relative frequency of multiple-activity households (those with four or more activities recorded).

Types of Activities in the Nonfarm Sector

Figure 3.2 presents generalized patterns of occupational structures of the rural nonfarm sector in Kenya, based on the frequency count in the first IRS Nonfarm Module. Additional detailed structural data are given in table 3.1. These data are in the form of occurrences of such activities in sampled households. It should be noted that recorded occurrences in households are not quite the same thing as simply a listing of sampled households in which nonfarm activities were recorded. This is because of the earlier-mentioned multiplicity of different nonfarm activities in some households. Therefore, in assessing the frequency of occurrence of different categories of activity, certain households may be counted more than once. An additional perspective on the regional significance of nonfarm activities is provided in figure 3.2 through the use of data on the provincial small-farm population taken from the *Integrated Rural Survey Basic Report 1974-75* (table 5.1 and figure 3.2).

Figure 3.2 illustrates the differences from province to province of particular nonfarm activities such as resource extraction which varies from about 2 percent of total cases in Central Province to over 10 percent in Nyanza, as well as construction, which varies from less than 1 percent in Central Province to more than 5 percent in Eastern Province. However, the dominance in all provinces of manufacturing as an activity category is noteworthy. It confirms that the nonfarm sector cannot merely be considered as a collection of essentially unproductive petty shopkeepers and traders. In Coast and Nyanza provinces, manufacturing activities account for more than 40 percent of total cases, and in only one province (Central Province) was the proportion less than 30 percent. Central Province has an exceptionally high incidence of households in which there were no recorded occurrences of nonfarm activities of any kind.

54

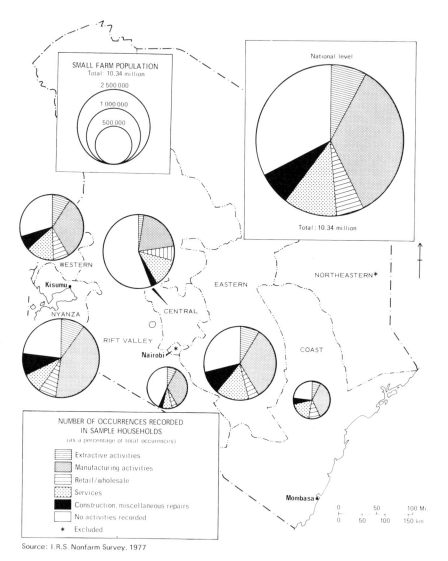

Source: I.R.S. Nonfarm Survey, 1977

Fig. 3.2 Patterns of Nonfarm activity and rural population in Kenya

Table 3.7 supplements the general overview of the structure of
rural nonfarm activities by providing a detailed breakdown of data
into specific kinds of activity recorded in national and provincial
sample households. Actual frequencies of recorded activities are
given as well as percentages which express the number of households
engaged in any specific activity as a ratio of the total number of
sample households. Once again, it should be noted that since many
households recorded more than one activity and others none at all,
the percentage figures for provinces do not sum to 100.

For the national sample as a whole, the most important
categories are: Manufacture of Food, Beverages, and Tobacco
Products (present in 22.3 percent of households), Total Services
(17.8 percent), Manufacture of Wood Products (14.0), Plant and
Animal Fiber Products and Wearing Apparel (12.4 percent), Resource
Extraction (12.1 percent), and Wholesale and Retail Trading (9.3
percent). Other categories are of relatively minor importance.
Thus, as might be expected, simple processing of local raw materials
and the provision of a wide range of "traditional" services such as
those dispensed by food kiosks, dancers, and traditional healers,
comprise the predominant part of the Kenyan rural nonfarm sector.
Relatively sophisticated forms of manufacturing and servicing are
not well represented in this sector.

A closer examination of individual types of activity in these
broad categories reveals that, in many cases, one or a few specific
activities account for the relative importance of the entire
category. For example, the brewing of *pombe,* a traditional
beverage, is clearly the most prevalent of all nonfarm activities in
sample households, and largely accounts for the prominence of the
whole Food, Beverage, and Tobacco Products sector.[6] Similarly, the
next highest ranking individual activities--charcoal making,
woodcutting, and duka (general store) operation--have an impact on
the relative importance of their respective activity categories.
Other important activities include several traditional cottage
industries, such as rope and basket making, and textile weaving or
knitting, as well as resource extraction occupations such as fishing
or hunting. In general, the data in table 3.7 attest to the
remarkable diversity of activities in the rural nonfarm sector.

A comparison of provincial activity structures is also
possible from the information in table 3.7. Summary percentage
figures for the broad categories in the six provinces reveal a
fairly consistent pattern in which Central Province, and to a

---

6. Since 1979, *pombe* brewing has been banned in Kenya.

TABLE 3.7

A DETAILED CLASSIFICATION OF NONFARM ACTIVITIES WITH
COMPARATIVE PROVINCIAL FREQUENCIES
(BASED ON I.R.S. NATIONAL HOUSEHOLD SURVEY
OF NONFARM ACTIVITIES, 1977)

Activity Category	Central		Coast		Eastern		Nyanza		Rift Valley		Western		National Level	
	No.	%	No.	%	No.	%	No.	%	No.	%	No.	%	No.	%
RESOURCE EXTRACTION														
Hunters	--	--	--	--	30	6.3	15	2.9	10	2.3	3	0.9	58	2.6
Gatherers of Forest Products and Beachcombers	--	--	7	5.6	1	0.2	7	1.4	5	1.1	4	1.2	24	1.1
Gatherers of Animal Manures	--	--	--	--	11	2.3	13	2.5	2	0.4	6	1.8	32	1.4
Wood Cutters	4	1.1	--	--	16	3.4	23	4.5	26	5.9	13	4.0	82	3.7
Bamboo and Reed Cutters	1	0.3	--	--	2	0.4	3	0.6	--	--	--	--	6	0.3
Fishermen	1	0.3	5	4.0	--	--	28	5.4	1	0.2	15	4.6	50	2.2
Sand and Gravel Quarrying	--	--	--	--	9	1.9	1	1.9	--	--	4	1.2	14	0.6
Other Quarrying, Mining or Prospecting	3	0.8	--	--	--	--	--	--	--	--	--	--	3	0.1
Total Resource Extraction	9	2.5	12	9.7	69	14.5	90	17.5	44	10.0	45	14.0	269	12.1

MANUFACTURING OF FOOD, BEVERAGES AND TOBACCO PRODUCTS

	No.	%	No.	%	No.	%	No.	%	No.	%	No.	%	Total No.	%
Posho Mills	2	0.6	—	—	1	0.2	6	1.2	10	2.3	3	0.9	22	1.0
Jaggery Mills	—	—	—	—	—	—	1	0.2	—	—	—	—	1	0.1
Bakeries	—	—	—	—	1	0.2	1	0.2	—	—	1	0.3	3	0.1
Butter and Cheese Making	—	—	—	—	—	—	7	1.4	—	—	—	—	7	0.3
Other Dairy Products	2	0.6	5	4.0	24	5.1	7	1.4	3	0.7	3	0.9	44	2.0
Coffee processing	3	0.8	—	—	11	2.3	3	0.6	—	—	—	—	17	0.8
Pombe Brewing	12	3.4	3	2.4	28	5.9	134	26.0	66	15.0	57	17.6	300	13.4
Other Drinks	—	—	14	11.3	—	—	19	3.7	3	0.7	11	3.4	47	2.1
Tobacco Products	1	0.3	1	0.8	21	4.4	2	0.4	7	1.6	6	1.8	38	1.7
Other Food Processing	1	0.3	7	5.6	1	0.2	8	1.6	1	0.2	—	—	18	0.8
Total Food Etc. Manufacture	21	5.9	30	24.2	87	18.3	188	36.5	90	20.5	81	25.1	497	22.3

MANUFACTURE OF PLANT AND ANIMAL FIBER PRODUCTS AND WEARING APPAREL

	No.	%	No.	%	No.	%	No.	%	No.	%	No.	%	Total No.	%
Sisal Bags and Mats	3	0.8	1	0.8	17	3.5	26	5.0	—	—	4	1.2	51	2.3
Reed and Rush Bags, Baskets and Mats	4	1.1	19	15.8	41	8.6	8	1.6	1	0.2	4	1.2	77	3.4
Weaving, Spinning, Knitting, Dyeing	1	0.3	4	3.2	22	4.6	13	2.5	19	4.3	10	3.1	69	3.1
Manufacture of Clothing, (tailors etc.)	6	1.7	1	0.8	8	1.7	9	1.7	3	0.7	1	0.3	28	1.2

TABLE 3.7, CONT.

Activity Category	Central No.	%	Coast No.	%	Eastern No.	%	Nyanza No.	%	Rift Valley No.	%	Western No.	%	National Level No.	%
Beadwork Necklaces and Other Jewelry	--	--	--	--	1	0.2	--	--	5	1.1	--	--	6	0.3
Preparation of Sheep-skins and Goatskins	--	--	--	--	2	0.4	3	0.6	26	5.9	1	0.3	32	1.4
Leather working (belts, bags, harness)	--	--	1	0.8	--	--	1	0.2	4	0.9	1	0.3	7	0.3
Shoes	1	0.3	--	--	2	0.4	1	0.2	--	--	1	0.3	5	0.2
Other Animal Skin products	--	--	--	--	--	--	2	0.4	--	--	--	--	2	0.1
Total Manufacture of Plant & Animal Fiber etc.	15	4.2	26	21.0	93	19.6	63	12.2	58	13.2	22	6.8	277	12.4
MANUFACTURE OF WOOD PRODUCTS														
Sawmills	6	1.7	--	--	1	0.2	4	0.8	2	0.4	1	0.3	14	0.6
Charcoal Making	24	6.7	2	1.6	34	7.2	31	6.0	32	7.3	13	4.0	136	6.1
Building Poles	1	0.3	1	0.8	10	2.1	10	1.9	4	0.9	3	0.9	29	1.3
Furniture	7	2.0	1	0.8	6	1.3	7	1.4	4	0.9	8	2.5	33	1.5
Wood Carvings	--	--	2	1.6	6	1.3	--	--	--	--	--	--	8	0.4
Wooden Handles for Tools, etc.	2	0.6	2	1.6	5	1.0	4	0.8	--	--	9	2.8	22	1.0
Other Wood Products	--	--	--	--	5	1.0	1	0.2	--	--	--	--	6	0.3

	C1 (n)	C1 (%)	C2 (n)	C2 (%)	C3 (n)	C3 (%)	C4 (n)	C4 (%)	C5 (n)	C5 (%)	C6 (n)	C6 (%)	Total (n)	Total (%)
Gourds and Calabashes	1	0.3	--	--	14	3.0	30	5.8	7	1.6	9	2.8	61	2.7
Containers and Crates	1	0.3	--	--	--	--	--	--	--	--	2	0.6	3	0.1
Total Wood Manufacture	42	11.8	8	6.4	81	17.0	87	16.9	49	11.2	45	14.0	312	14.0
POTTERY PRODUCTS														
Pottery Plates, Bowls, Pots, etc.	--	--	1	0.8	5	1.0	28	5.4	1	0.2	3	0.9	38	1.7
Total Pottery	--	--	1	0.8	5	1.0	28	5.4	1	0.2	3	0.9	38	1.7
MANUFACTURE OF METAL PRODUCTS														
Blacksmith	2	0.6	1	0.8	--	--	2	0.4	--	--	1	0.3	6	0.3
Farm Implements and Tools	--	--	--	--	1	0.2	1	0.2	--	--	1	0.3	3	0.1
Household Utensils (Jikos, Pans, etc.)	4	1.1	--	--	4	0.8	5	1.0	3	0.7	2	0.6	18	0.8
Total Metal Manufacture	6	1.7	1	0.8	5	1.0	8	1.6	3	0.7	4	1.2	27	1.2
CONSTRUCTION														
Manufacture of Cement Blocks	--	--	--	--	2	0.4	6	1.2	--	--	--	--	8	0.4
Stone Building Blocks	2	0.6	1	0.8	4	0.8	6	1.2	2	0.4	2	0.6	17	0.8
Other Building Materials, e.g. Hard Core, Bricks, etc.	1	0.3	--	--	23	4.8	8	1.6	--	--	5	1.5	37	1.6

TABLE 3.7, CONT.

Activity Category	Central		Coast		Eastern		Nyanza		Rift Valley		Western		National Level	
	No.	%	No.	%	No.	%	No.	%	No.	%	No.	%	No.	%
Building and Construction	--	--	2	1.6	16	3.4	15	2.9	2	0.4	8	2.5	43	1.9
Total Construction														
WHOLESALE AND RETAIL TRADING														
Wholesale Trading	4	1.1	--	--	2	0.4	7	1.4	--	--	--	--	13	0.6
Agents (Selling on Commission)	1	0.3	2	1.6	--	--	7	1.4	--	--	1	0.3	11	0.5
Clothing Vendors	3	0.8	--	--	2	0.4	5	1.0	1	0.2	--	--	11	0.5
Dukas (General Retailers)	12	3.4	1	0.8	19	4.0	20	3.8	14	3.2	16	5.0	82	3.7
Butchers	4	1.1	1	0.8	9	1.9	11	2.1	9	2.0	8	2.5	42	1.9
Specialized Retail Stores	--	--	1	0.8	--	--	--	--	--	--	--	--	1	0.1
Petrol Stations	--	--	--	--	1	0.2	--	--	--	--	--	--	1	0.1
Hawkers and Itinerant Vendors	1	0.3	2	1.6	1	0.2	8	1.6	2	0.4	9	2.8	23	1.0
Dealers in Secondhand Goods/Junk	1	0.3	--	--	2	0.4	4	0.8	--	--	2	0.6	9	0.4
Retailing or Selling	--	--	1	0.8	2	0.4	8	1.6	--	--	3	0.9	14	0.6
Total Wholesale/Retail	26	7.3	8	6.4	38	8.0	70	13.7	26	5.9	39	12.1	207	9.3

REPAIRING

	n	%	n	%	n	%	n	%	n	%	n	%	Total n	Total %
Bicycle Repair	--	--	2	1.6	6	1.3	6	1.2	2	0.4	1	0.3	17	0.8
Motor Car and Truck Repairs	2	0.6	--	--	2	0.4	7	1.4	1	0.2	4	1.2	16	0.7
Repair of Other Vehicles	--	--	--	--	2	0.4	2	0.4	--	--	--	--	4	0.2
Farm Machinery and Tool Repairs	1	0.3	--	--	2	0.4	--	--	1	0.2	2	0.6	3	0.1
Household Utensil Repairs	--	--	1	0.8	2	0.4	11	2.1	2	0.4	3	0.9	6	0.3
Furniture Repairs	3	0.8	--	--	9	1.9	6	1.2	1	0.2	5	1.5	28	1.2
Shoes and Footwear Repairs	--	--	1	0.8	9	1.9	13	2.5	4	0.9	3	0.9	22	1.0
Clothing Repairs and Mending	5	1.4	--	--	7	1.5	1	0.2	--	--	2	0.6	32	1.4
Other Repairing and Renovating	--	--	--	--	--	--	--	--	--	--	--	--	3	0.1
Total Repairing	11	3.1	4	3.2	39	8.2	46	8.9	11	2.5	20	6.2	131	5.4

SERVICES: TRANSPORT, STORAGE AND COMMUNICATION

	n	%	n	%	n	%	n	%	n	%	n	%	Total n	Total %
Country Bus Operators	--	--	--	--	1	0.2	1	0.2	--	--	--	--	2	0.1
Matatu Taxi Operators	7	2.0	--	--	5	1.0	2	0.4	3	0.7	5	1.5	22	1.0
Water Carriers	2	0.6	--	--	18	3.7	1	0.2	--	--	1	0.3	22	1.0
Truck & Lorry Operators	4	1.1	--	--	6	1.3	--	--	3	0.7	2	0.6	15	0.7
Other Transport Operators	2	0.6	--	--	2	0.4	--	--	4	0.9	6	1.8	14	0.6
Messenger Services	--	--	4	3.2	--	--	5	1.0	5	1.1	--	--	14	0.6

TABLE 3.7, CONT.

Activity Category	Central No.	%	Coast No.	%	Eastern No.	%	Nyanza No.	%	Rift Valley No.	%	Western No.	%	National Level No.	%
Storage for Agricultural or Other Produce	--	--	--	--	--	--	2	0.4	--	--	1	0.3	3	0.1
Total Transport etc.	15	4.3	4	3.2	32	6.6	11	2.2	15	3.4	15	4.5	92	4.1
SERVICES: ACCOMMODATION, FOOD AND BEVERAGE SERVICES														
Cafes, Restaurants	--	--	--	--	1	0.2	--	--	--	--	--	--	1	0.1
Food Kiosks	4	1.1	--	--	2	0.4	14	2.7	2	0.4	1	0.3	23	1.0
Meat Roasters	2	0.6	--	--	7	1.5	1	0.2	1	0.2	2	0.6	13	0.6
Bars	4	1.1	--	--	12	2.5	3	0.6	1	0.2	2	0.6	22	1.0
Hotels	3	0.8	--	--	21	4.4	5	1.0	4	0.9	2	0.6	35	1.6
Lodging or Boarding Homes	1	0.3	--	--	5	1.0	1	0.2	--	--	--	--	7	0.3
Total Accommodation etc.	14	3.9	--	--	48	10.0	24	4.7	8	1.7	7	2.1	100	4.6
SERVICES: FINANCIAL INSURANCE AND BUSINESS SERVICES														
Money Lenders	2	0.6	2	1.6	--	--	2	0.4	--	--	--	--	6	0.3
Renting of Goods & Equipment	--	--	--	--	1	0.2	1	0.2	--	--	--	--	2	0.1

	1 No.	1 %	2 No.	2 %	3 No.	3 %	4 No.	4 %	5 No.	5 %	6 No.	6 %	Total No.	Total %
Letter Writers	1	0.3	--	--	1	0.2	--	--	2	0.4	--	--	4	0.2
Translators	--	--	11	8.9	--	--	2	0.4	--	--	--	--	13	0.6
Total Financial etc.	3	0.9	13	10.5	2	0.4	5	1.0	2	0.4	--	--	25	1.2
SERVICES: COMMUNITY, SOCIAL AND PERSONAL SERVICES														
Educational Services	--	--	1	0.8	4	0.8	--	--	1	0.2	1	0.3	7	0.3
Midwives	--	--	1	0.8	5	1.0	--	--	1	0.2	1	0.3	8	0.4
Clinics	--	--	--	--	1	0.2	1	0.2	3	0.7	--	--	5	0.2
Traditional Healers	--	--	6	4.8	12	2.5	21	4.1	2	0.4	6	1.8	47	2.1
Pest Exterminators	--	--	--	--	2	0.4	--	--	--	--	--	--	2	0.1
Undertakers	2	0.6	2	1.6	6	1.3	2	0.4	1	0.2	1	0.3	12	0.5
Dancers, Entertainers	--	--	1	0.8	1	0.2	3	0.6	13	3.0	2	0.6	22	1.0
Laundry (Cleaners)	--	--	1	0.8	--	--	3	0.6	--	--	--	--	4	0.2
Barbers/Hairdressers	--	--	--	--	--	--	--	--	1	0.2	3	0.9	4	0.2
Shoeshine Services	--	--	--	--	2	0.4	--	--	--	--	--	--	2	0.1
Astrologers	--	--	1	0.8	--	--	--	--	--	--	2	0.6	3	0.1
Total Community etc.	2	0.6	13	10.4	33	6.8	30	5.9	22	4.9	16	4.8	116	5.2
Other Services	17	4.8	1	0.8	9	1.9	4	0.8	1	0.2	31	9.6	63	2.8
Total Services	51	14.3	31	25.0	124	26.2	74	14.7	48	10.9	69	21.4	397	17.8

TABLE 3.7, CONT.

Activity Category	Central No.	%	Coast No.	%	Eastern No.	%	Nyanza No.	%	Rift Valley No.	%	Western No.	%	National Level No.	%
TOTAL ALL CATEGORIES	184	*	126	*	586	*	689	*	334	*	343	*	2260	*

* Does not sum to 100% due to multiple occurrences of activites in some households.

% Occurrences as percent of households.

NOTE: The following activity categories employed in the original survey were found to contain zero frequencies in all provinces: Lime making; Tarpaulins, Tents and Canvas Goods; Bags and Sacks for Maize and Produce; Other Ornaments and Apparel; Glass Products; Carved Kisii Stone Ware; Other Metal Products; Dealers in Automobile Spare Parts; Other Machinery Repairs; Maize Roasters; Other Financial or Business Services.

certain extent Rift Valley Province, are shown to be distinctly
different from Nyanza, Western, and Eastern Provinces, with Coast
Province falling into the middle ground. In most cases, Central
Province records the lowest percentage for various activity
categories, with one or two notable exceptions (such as in Metal
Products Manufacturing where it ranks highest), but even here its
distinctiveness is preserved. Rift Valley tends to follow a similar
pattern. Conversely, Western, Nyanza, and Eastern provinces
generally rank highest on many of the broad activity categories
listed, indicating that such occupations are more prevalent in these
provinces than elsewhere.

A number of nonfarm activities show interesting regional
patterns. For the most part, the distribution of resource
extraction activities is governed by the availability of resources.
Thus hunting, the gathering of forest products, and woodcutting, all
of which tend to be related to the presence of forest and bush, are
poorly represented in the Central and Coast provinces. Kenya's
fishing industry is found mainly along the Indian Ocean littoral and
on Lake Nyanza (Victoria).

The distribution of food product industries is largely
governed by the location of pombe brewing which accounts for 60
percent of the frequency in this category. Pombe brewing is fairly
evenly distributed across all of the provinces except Central
Province. The major wood product industry is charcoal burning which
occurs frequently in all provinces except the Coast. The pottery
industry is highly concentrated in Nyanza Province. Construction
shows a curious concentration in Nyanza and Eastern provinces, but
the manufacture of metal products, wholesaling and retailing,
repairing and other services, all display a fairly even
distribution, though with certain specific exceptions such as the
concentration of water carriers in Eastern Province. It will be
noted that accommodation, food, and beverage services were not
encountered in the Coast sample.

Nonfarm Employment Structure

Additional data on nonfarm sector employment characteristics
were obtained in the second IRS Nonfarm Survey Model, conducted in
1977-78. Features of this survey are discussed in the Appendix. The
data relate to the age and sex of workers in nonfarm activities at
the national level (table 3.8), family participation in household
nonfarm enterprises (table 3.9), wage workers and unpaid employees
(table 3.10), and educational/literacy characteristics of nonfarm
workers (table 3.11).

66

TABLE 3.8

PARTICIPATION BY WOMEN AND YOUNG
ADULTS IN THE NONFARM SECTOR:
PROVINCIAL COMPARISONS
(Response Frequency: 527)

| | Provinces | | | | | | National |
	Central	Coast	Eastern	Nyanza	Rift	Western	
Women in Nonfarm Activities (percent)	29.0	9.3	25.7	28.7	6.9	11.3	19.0
Operators under 30 years (percent)	34.2	49.3	26.7	32.3	42.6	29.0	36.2

SOURCE: IRS Nonfarm Module 2, 1977-78. (Unpublished.)

NOTE: Row totals may not add exactly to 100% due to rounding. Nairobi and Northeastern provinces are excluded from the survey.

TABLE 3.9

FAMILIES OF HOUSEHOLD HEADS OPERATING NONFARM ENTERPRISES:
PROVINCIAL COMPARISONS (Response Frequency: 527)

| | Provinces | | | | | | National |
	Central	Coast	Eastern	Nyanza	Rift	Western	
Percent wives of Household Head engaged in RNFA	18.4	5.3	9.9	20.6	5.2	4.8	11.0
Percent children of Household Head engaged in RNFA	7.9	13.3	10.9	9.6	6.1	11.3	9.7

SOURCE: IRS Nonfarm Module 2, 1977-78. (Unpublished.)

Age and Sex of Nonfarm Workers

Table 3.8 reveals the mostly youthful character of workers in the nonfarm sector: at the national level, over 36.2 percent are under thirty years of age, compared to 30.8 percent for the rural population as a whole in the age group from 15 to 39 years. It is possible that this represents the beginnings of a new landless class of rural residents in the ranks of recent school leavers. Nonetheless, some young entrepreneurs will undoubtedly inherit land eventually from aging parents. More will be said about this pattern later.

In clear contrast to the pattern in other parts of Africa, notably West Africa, the majority of workers in the nonfarm sector in Kenya are males. Females represent under a fifth of all workers in this sector, with the proportion rising to over a quarter in Central, Eastern, and Nyanza provinces (table 3.10). Coast and Rift Valley have remarkably low proportions of women in the nonfarm sector, in both cases under ten percent. Since most jobs for women in the nonfarm sector are in vending or retailing of farm produce, it is probable that the variation in the participation of women is related to the prosperity of smallfarming: crop surpluses from the farm are taken to market and sold by the womenfolk, who may also have the time for making crafts for sale in the market place. Alternately, if the farmer is a successful entrepreneur, farm handicrafts may be sold in a duka which the farmer's wife may manage on his behalf. In farming areas where no surpluses of fruit and vegetables are available for cash sale or where women cannot be spared from farm duties on a regular basis to tend a nonfarm business, the proportion of female entrepreneurs is lower.

More light on this question is provided by the data in table 3.9 where it is shown that, at a national scale, 11 percent of nonfarm entrepreneurs are the wives of household heads. Relative to the proportions of women in the nonfarm sector, wives of household heads are more prominent in Rift Valley, Nyanza, and Central provinces. But from table 3.9 it will be noted that nearly ten percent of all nonfarm entrepreneurs are children of the household head and that the province with the highest proportion of children of household heads is also the province with the greatest proportion of entrepreneurs under thirty years of age (i.e., Coast Province). The correlation between age and relation to head of household is not strong for all other provinces, however.

Ownership, Wage Employment, and Unpaid Work

The rural nonfarm sector, like the urban informal sector, is characterized by a large proportion of small, owner-operated businesses. At the national level, according to the data from the second IRS Nonfarm module, 44 percent of all workers in the sector are owners or managers of their own or a family business. Conversely, 56 percent are wage employees and unpaid workers (table 3.10) including 38 percent of all workers who are in government employment or similar occupations. Workers in the rural nonfarm sector could not, therefore, by any stretch of the imagination be described as a proletariat of wage workers. They are more aptly described as a cadre of entrepreneurs and owners or managers of family businesses. Again, there is strong interprovincial variation in the proportions of wage employees in the sector. Coast and Rift Valley have the highest percentages and also have the highest proportions of young workers in the nonfarm sector (Compare tables 3.8 and 3.10). Central and Nyanza have markedly lower percentages

TABLE 3.10

NONFARM WAGE AND UNPAID EMPLOYMENT:

PROVINCIAL COMPARISONS

(Response Frequency: 527)

	Provinces						National
	Central	Coast	Eastern	Nyanza	Rift	Western	
Percent NFA in wage employment	36.8	85.3	47.5	39.7	70.4	56.4	56.0
Percent NFA unpaid workers	0.0	2.7	1.0	4.4	1.7	0.0	2.1

SOURCE: IRS Nonfarm Module 2, 1977-78. (Unpublished.)

of wage workers.

Literacy and Education of Workers

Available data suggest that, on the whole, workers in the rural nonfarm sector are far better educated than the average rural resident. Table 3.11 reveals that 15 percent of nonfarm workers had some high school education, as against only 1.6 percent of the rural

small farm population in the "17 years plus" age bracket. The data
show that Central Province has the best educated rural population,
in terms of the proportion of the total population having some high
school education, whereas Rift Valley has the lowest rate of high
school education among its small farm population in general. Yet,
Rift Valley is shown as having the highest proportion of its nonfarm
workers with some secondary schooling, even higher than Central
Province. In contrast, four provinces--Nyanza, Western, Coast, and
Eastern--stand out as having the highest proportion of illiterate
workers in nonfarm activities (i.e., those who are unable to write
in their own dialect). The data on education are thus somewhat
ambiguous; despite the relatively high educational attainment of a
significant minority of nonfarm workers, it remains apparent that a
general inability to write in local dialects or the national
business languages, to keep records, or to negotiate business
dealings in a more formal manner will remain a key aspect of the
rural nonfarm sector for some time to come. If, as some writers
claim, the nonfarm sector is composed of a new petty bourgeoisie, it

TABLE 3.11

EDUCATION AND LITERACY IN THE NONFARM SECTOR:
PROVINCIAL COMPARISONS
(Response Frequency: 527)

	Provinces						National
	Central	Coast	Eastern	Nyanza	Rift	Western	
Percent with some high school education	15.8	13.3	9.6	14.7	20.9	9.7	15.0
Percent illiterate (cannot write own dialect)	28.9	40.0	34.6	40.4	25.2	37.1	34.3

SOURCE: IRS Nonfarm Module 2, 1977-78.   (Unpublished.)

is to some degree an illiterate one.

From the above series of tables, a pattern of interprovincial
variation in the character of the rural nonfarm sector emerges which
suggests that the sector performs quite different economic and
social roles in different parts of Kenya. For example, the majority

of nonfarm workers in Rift Valley Province are young single men with
some high school education. Few are illiterate in their own
dialect, female, or the spouses or children of the head of their
household. By contrast, in Eastern Province, nonfarm workers are
much more likely to be older, without high school education--perhaps
even illiterate--and to be the owner or manager of an enterprise.
The possibility must be examined that such interprovincial contrasts
reflect different provincial nonfarm activity structures. This we
do in the following section with the aid of more detailed tables.

Employment Structure

Table 3.12 provides a national overview of the pattern of
nonfarm sector characteristics, based on the Second IRS Nonfarm
Survey module. These are disaggregated into classes of principal
nonfarm activity in which the respondents were actively engaged at
the time of the survey. Of the thirteen categories, two stand out
as disproportionally large; "other activities", with 200
respondents, and "wholesale/retail" with 104 respondents. Some
comments must be made on these two categories at the outset. The
category of "other activities" comprises mostly formal sector
(largely government) workers. This category had been excluded from
the earlier IRS Survey. The large number of wholesale and retail
workers is partly due to inclusion in this category of employees in
bars, restaurants, and hotels (these were placed in a separate
category in the first IRS Survey discussed earlier). It is clear
from the data that trading and vending of all types comprise a very
important subsector of the rural nonfarm sector.

It would be far from the truth, however, to claim that the
nonfarm sector is simply another name for petty trading and
shopkeeping and therefore is basically nonproductive in a strict
sense. Table 3.12 makes abundantly clear that manufacturing and
processing activities are also a highly significant component of the
nonfarm sector. Agroprocessing, that is, the conversion of farm
produce or other materials from field or forest into forms that are
more valuable and usable, alone comprises more than 16 percent. As
shown in table 3.12 this subsector makes many jobs available for
women, especially for those who must work part of the time on the
family farm, and who are less likely to be literate. The same is
true for the resource extraction subsector, which also has an
affinity for part-time farmers and their families (i.e. those who
are engaged for one or more days per week in farm work).

TABLE 3.12

NONFARM ACTIVITY STRUCTURES AND EMPLOYMENT
CHARACTERISTICS: NATIONAL LEVEL, 1977

Activity	% wage employees	% female workers	% with high school	% with 1+ days farm work	% full time 5+ days	% literacy Swahili and English	Response Frequency
1. Resource Extraction	33.3	14.8	27.8	66.7	42.6	27.8	54
2. Food, Beverage and Tobacco Products	38.3	44.7	29.8	53.2	51.1	19.2	47
3. Fiber Prod. and Clothing	21.7	43.5	26.1	73.9	43.5	34.8	23
4. Wood Prods.	25.0	0.0	50.0	45.0	65.0	35.0	20
5. Metal Prods.	0.0	0.0	33.3	33.3	66.7	0.0	3
6. Other Manuf'g.	45.5	54.5	0.0	72.7	36.4	9.1	11
7. Construction & Building Mats	55.6	0.0	33.3	66.7	66.7	22.2	9
8. Wholesale/ Retail	20.2	17.3	45.2	60.6	58.6	41.3	104
9. Repairing	20.0	0.0	60.0	50.0	90.0	50.0	10
10. Transport & Storage	70.4	11.1	40.7	14.8	74.1	48.1	27
11. Services: Financial	100.0	20.0	40.0	20.0	100.0	40.0	5
12. Services: Community	46.2	15.4	38.5	38.5	61.5	53.8	13
13. Other Activities (Public Sector)	91.0	16.5	66.5	44.0	79.5	66.0	200
Response Frequency	291	102	253	268	344	244	527

SOURCE: IRS Nonfarm Module 2, 1977-78. (Unpublished.)

Relatively few workers are engaged in metal product manufacture in rural Kenya, and this at first may appear to be a subsector ripe for expansion. But several points about this sector must be borne in mind. First, the raw materials for this sector are often derived from the modern sector in the form of scrap metal, oil-drums, automobile leaf springs, and the like. The size of the sector is regulated to some extent by the "trickle down" of materials from the modern sector. Second, considerable metallurgical skill and equipment are required to manufacture any but the simplest of metal products, and this acts to limit the unaided entry of rural entrepreneurs to this sector. Third, mass-produced metal products manufactured overseas or in Nairobi are more likely to displace locally-produced metal products from the markets of rural Kenya than is the case with fiber or wood products, for example. These factors help to explain the small size of the metal working sector. It will be noticed in this subsector and the allied construction sector that there are minimal numbers of female workers and that the proportions of full-time workers are higher than in the agroprocessing categories.

Repairing, transportation, and services constitute another important group of activities in the nonfarm sector which generates considerable wage employment--but mostly for males--and which comprises mostly full-time operatives. In these service activities, again as one might expect, the level of literacy in the business languages is higher than average.

Incomes in the Rural Nonfarm Sector

National income patterns for the various classes of nonfarm activity are presented in table 3.13. The highest incomes (outside of public sector jobs) are earned in the service and wholesale/retail categories. Indeed, certain types of service activities in the nonfarm sector pay incomes that are nearly equivalent to public sector salaries. But in many other cases incomes are considerably lower.

Nonfarm activities in the "middle income" range include transport, construction, wood and metal manufacturing, and food processing. The lowest average incomes in the rural nonfarm sector appear to be associated with extractive activities such as fishing and trapping and with cottage crafts like rope making, basket weaving or miscellaneous manufacturing. Repairing is also a low-income occupation in rural Kenya. As noted previously, these activities tend to attract large numbers of part-time workers who

73

TABLE 3.13

AVERAGE INCOME (KShs. PER PERSON PER MONTH)

Activity Groups	Response Frequency	National Average Income (KShs.)
1. Resource Extraction	54	204
2. Food, Beverages and Tobacco Products	47	345
3. Fiber Products and Clothing	23	210
4. Wood Products	20	400
5. Metal Products	3	373
6. Other Manufacturing	11	149
7. Construction Building Materials	9	416
8. Wholesale and Retail	104	422
9. Repairing	10	299
10. Transport and Storage	27	344
11. Financial Services	5	477
12. Community Services	13	468
13. Other (Public Sector)	200	506
National Level	527	403

SOURCE: Second IRS Nonfarm Module, 1977-78. (Unpublished.)

are supplementing family farm income or earnings from other nonfarm occupations. The reason for the continued interest by most Kenyan job-seekers in the public sector is apparent from table 3.13, but so too is the fact that certain types of rural nonfarm activity can pay almost equivalent returns to employees.

Besides being characterized by broad variations in income among activity types, there are also substantial variations amongst the provinces, with Eastern and Western provinces below the national average and Central Province being well above (table 3.14). It appears that the level of incomes in the rural nonfarm sector mirrors the general level of agricultural prosperity and development in Kenya's rural regions as a whole. More will be said about the implications of this relationship between farm and nonfarm sectors

TABLE 3.14

REGIONAL VARIATIONS IN NONFARM INCOME

Province	Response Frequency	Average Nonfarm Sector Income (KShs)
Central	39	461
Coast	74	425
Eastern	101	329
Nyanza	136	405
Rift	116	437
Western	61	394
National	527	403

SOURCE: Second IRS Nonfarm Module, 1977-78. (Unpublished.)

in a later chapter.

Sectoral Variation and the Individual Enterprise

The above discussion has served to highlight the prevalence of nonfarm activities in rural Kenya, both in market centers and on farmsteads, as well as revealing a highly varied occupational and regional structure. The part-time nature of many activities is also notable. Much of the foregoing discussion points to the nonfarm *enterprise* as a basic unit of organization in this economic sector. To gain a better understanding of the operation of this basic unit, we provide in the next chapter a detailed case study of nonfarm enterprises in Central Province.

CHAPTER IV

CHARACTERISTICS OF NONFARM ENTERPRISES
AND ENTREPRENEURS: A CASE STUDY
FROM CENTRAL PROVINCE

The objective of this case study is to explore both the
operating characteristics of rural nonfarm enterprises and the
background of the people who operate them. Facets of the
enterprises to be examined include ownership, enterprise size and
mobility, employment, productivity characteristics, capitalization,
competitiveness, and (by way of an introduction to later chapters in
this study) enterprise linkages, with their geographical as well as
economic implications. First, however, we must set the stage for
the discussion by outlining the characteristics of the Central
Province region and of the survey from which the basic data are
drawn.

The Regional Setting: Central Province

In terms of area, Central Province is one of the smallest of
Kenya's eight provinces, but it is also one of the most densely
populated. Its 13,000 square kilometers of land are home to more
than three million Kikuyu farmers and townsmen. The province is
located in the fertile highlands to the east of the Great Rift
Valley (figure 4.1). On its southern flanks are the city of Nairobi
and the Masai grazing lands of Ndeiya. To the north and northeast
are the ranches of the Laikipia district and the forested slopes of
Mt. Kenya. Parts of these bordering areas were once in the European
enclave of the White Highlands, and other parts are the homelands of
the Embu and Meru peoples. To the east the land slopes down to the
semi-arid nyika occupied mainly by Kamba peoples. Three zones
within the Kikuyu homeland are usually identified: High Kikuyu,
Middle Kikuyu, and Low Kikuyu with boundaries determined by
rainfall, elevation, and agricultural characteristics.[1] Peasant
small holdings located mainly in High and Middle Kikuyu produce a
variety of cash and subsistence crops such as coffee, tea,

---

1. D.R. Fraser Taylor, "The Internal Trade of Fort Hall District, Kenya,"
Canadian Journal of African Studies 1 (1967): 111-122.

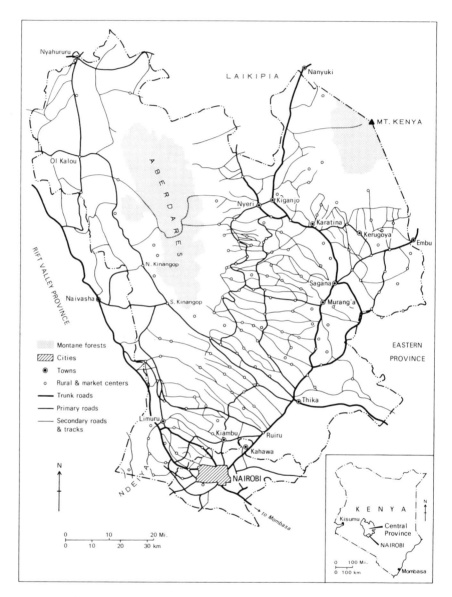

Fig. 4.1 Patterns of settlement and transportation in Central Province

pyrethrum, maize, beans, and tropical fruit. Livestock assume
increasing importance in the more arid areas of Low Kikuyu to the
east and northwest. High and Middle Kikuyu appear to be the more
prosperous areas, with denser settlement and more agricultural
surplus. The land area in these sub-regions is deeply dissected by
ridge and gorge topography which has a pronounced
northwest-southeast trend. The effect of physiography on settlement
and transportation patterns is obvious (figure 4.1).

The Central Province Survey Data

The case studies in this chapter are based on data drawn from
a survey of nonfarm activities conducted by the authors in 1977.
Specifics of this survey are to be found in the Appendix. It should
be noted that the survey covered nonfarm enterprises in selected
market centers (see figure 4.2) but did not include those activities
conducted on dispersed rural farmsteads. Hence the conclusions
reached about the nature of enterprises in Central Province need to
be qualified with the cautionary note that the numerous dispersed
forms of nonfarm enterprise have not been included. Even so, a
sample of fully 852 enterprises was surveyed in considerable detail,
these being selected from 52 small rural market centers on the basis
of a sampling frame that took into consideration rural population
density and the periodic nature of many of the market centers in
Central Province. Figure 4.3 gives details of market periodicity in
sampled marketplaces, distinguishes their special market days, and
identifies non-periodic (i.e., daily-operating) markets. The
predominance of the bi-weekly markets and daily markets in the
Central Province system is evident.

Age and Ownership of Nonfarm Enterprises

Most of the enterprises interviewed were fairly new with a
mean age of 6 years. The distribution was skewed, however, by the
presence of a few that were long-established; indeed, one was
founded in 1930. The median enterprise was 3 years old, while the
modal class was only 1 year old. Clearly, most of the enterprises
were quite newly established, and although some had risen
phoenix-like from the ashes of failed enterprises, others were
totally new. The overall impression is one of quite rapid expansion
in this sector. The Government's drive to "Kenyanize" business
coupled with the relative prosperity of the mid-1970s (especially in
the 1976-77 coffee boom) were factors in this expansion.

Female participation in the operation of the nonfarm sector is
quite high and almost certainly higher than in the formal sector.

78

Fig. 4.2   Location of selected market centers

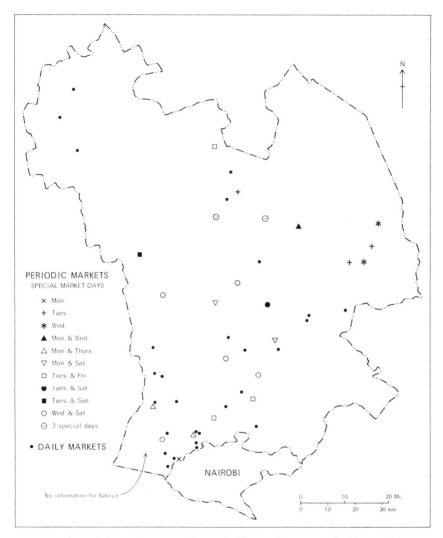

Fig. 4.3 Patterns of periodic and non-periodic markets
in the Central Province sample

One-quarter of the interviewees were female. Table 4.1, giving the
breakdown by sex of interviewee for the main activity groups, shows
a higher level of female participation in dukas and other vending
(mainly fruit and vegetable selling), and a not-unexpected low level
in wood and metal fabrication, petrol stations and repair shops, and

TABLE 4.1

MALE/FEMALE PARTICIPATION RATES IN MAJOR ACTIVITY GROUPS

Activity Group	Percent of Interviewees		Number of Interviewee
	Male	Female	
1. Primary Extraction and Food Industries	84.1	15.9	46
2. Textiles and Clothing	73.8	26.2	84
3. Wood and Metal Fabrication	96.4	3.6	55
4. Dukas	64.4	35.6	208
5. Hotels, Bars, and Restaurants	81.8	18.2	110
6. Butchery and Meat Roasters	75.4	24.6	61
7. Other Vending	59.1	40.9	159
8. Petrol Stations and Repair Shops	96.0	4.0	50
9. Other Services	92.2	7.8	75
Total	74.9	25.1	848

SOURCE: Central Province Nonfarm Enterprise Survey, 1977.

in other services.

Tables 4.2 and 4.3 reveal other demographic characteristics of
the owners or operators of nonfarm businesses. It is clear that, in
Central Province, enterprise operators are a much younger group than
the farming population as a whole, with a concentration of
respondents in the under-thirty age group. As might be expected
with such a youthful group of entrepreneurs, family size of
respondents tends to be smaller than the average rural family: over
fifty percent have four or fewer children in an area where the
average household size is around seven persons.[2] It is not clear,
however, whether this is due simply to the factor of youthfulness or
whether the nonfarm activity itself is responsible for smaller
family size. It is possible that, just a urban families are smaller

2. Republic of Kenya, Central Bureau of Statistics, *Integrated Rural
Survey: Basic Report 1974-75* (Nairobi: Government Printer, 1977), p. 32.

than farm families owing to the economic and social circumstances in
cities, smaller nonfarm families in market centers may be the result

TABLE 4.2

AGE DISTRIBUTION OF RESPONDENTS COMPARED WITH SMALL FARM
DWELLERS IN CENTRAL PROVINCE IN 1974

	Age Group						Total
	15-19	20-29	30-39	40-49	50-59	60+	
Enterprise Survey	2.3	32.6	30.1	29.8	9.0	6.2	100.0
Small Farm Population, Central Province, 1974	18.0	20.8	16.8	13.6	11.8	19.0	100.0

SOURCE: Central Bureau of Statistics, Ministry of Finance and Planning,
Integrated Rural Survey 1974-75: Basic Report (Nairobi, 1977), table 5.2, p. 24.

TABLE 4.3

FAMILY SIZE OF RESPONDENTS

Number of Children	Frequency	percent
0	138	16.2
1	49	5.8
2	81	9.5
3	88	10.3
4	95	11.2
5	75	8.8
6	94	11.0
7	55	6.5
8+	177	20.8

SOURCE: Central Province Nonfarm Enterprise Survey, 1977.

of similar economic and social influences.

The age distribution of operators themselves, as table 4.2
confirms, tended to be concentrated in the 20-40 year age groups.
Very few were under 20 years, and only fifteen percent were aged 50
or more. Comparing the age distribution of the operators with that
of the small farm population in Central Province aged over 15, it is
clear that proportionately fewer old people were operating nonfarm

enterprises. Eighteen percent of the operators were not married, mainly those in the younger age groups. Interestingly, a number of interviewees remarked that they had delayed marriage because of their responsibilities in the enterprise. Despite the generally small family size noted above, great variations were apparent in the respondents' number of children (table 4.3). One respondent in eight had nine or more children, one in six had no children. The remainder were spread over the range from 1 to 8 children with a slightly higher frequency having 3 to 6 children.

As regards business proprietorship, three-quarters of the enterprises were established by the interviewee, either as owner or as part-owner. The remaining one-quarter were established by someone other than the interviewee who, in such cases, was invariably a hired manager. Typically, these managers had joined the enterprise within the previous two years, which suggests a fair degree of job mobility.

Half of the other partners in enterprises owned by partnerships were related to the operator, while 60 percent of the managers were related to the owner (often they were wives). Thus less than 10 percent of the enterprise operators had no familial ties with the owners. Family ties were important also in the selection of sub-contractors. About 20 percent of rural manufacturers sub-contracted work, mainly within the same sub-location, and commonly to relatives. Relatives also play important roles as suppliers of inputs and as customers. Moreover, many wage employees are related to the owner or manager of an enterprise, while some owners make use of large inputs of unpaid family help. In short, family connections are a very important part of the system.

Enterprise Size and Mobility

Rural enterprises in Central Province are extremely small. Two thirds of the sampled enterprises in market centers were single-person operations, and the average number of paid employees (including the operator) across all enterprises was 1.8. In only five activities was the average workforce in an enterprise greater than three employees, namely: dairies, pombe breweries, sawmills, petrol stations, and car repairing operations. Table 4.4 gives some details of employment in Central Province nonfarm enterprises. For instance, there were 9 establishments with 5 or more skilled employees. Fruit and vegetable selling, dukas, butchers, and clothing vendors were, in contrast, overwhelmingly one-person

TABLE 4.4

NUMBER OF EMPLOYEES IN CENTRAL PROVINCE NONFARM ENTERPRISES
BY TYPE OF EMPLOYMENT

Number of Employees Per Establishment	Establishments Employing:				
	Skilled Employees	Semi-Skilled Employees	Apprentices	Non-Production Employees (e.g., clerical)	Part-time Employees
1	97	37	23	3	38
2	49	25	9	0	19
3	12	4	3	0	10
4	9	3	0	0	1
5 or more	9	9	1	0	5
Total number of Establishments	176	78	36	3	73

SOURCE: Central Province Nonfarm Enterprise Survey, 1977.

NOTE: The number of employees excludes the operator/owner.

operations. Just over half of the paid employees were fulltime
skilled workers, one-quarter were semi-skilled. The remainder were
apprentices or part-time employees, with virtually no non-production
(e.g., office) employees being recorded.

It would be misleading, however, to leave the impression that
no unpaid help is given in many of these one person operations.
Well over a quarter of the enterprises, mainly those with no
employees, receive unpaid family help varying from 1 hour to 210
hours per week, with a mean of 40 hours for the 240 establishments.[3]
This average of 40 hours is close to being the equivalent of a full
working week for one employee, which indicates the magnitude of this
input of unpaid help. Indeed, since 240 establishments are
involved, the total input of unpaid family help is greater than the
paid input of semi-skilled labor. This result is, curiously, in
contrast with the national pattern reported in chapter 3.

---

3. Glen B. Norcliffe and Donald B. Freeman, *Nonfarm Activities in Market
Centres of Central Province, Kenya* (Toronto: York University Department of
Geography, Kenya Rural Nonfarm Sector Project, Research Report no. 3, 1979), p.
28.

Enterprises in the market centers can be classified according to whether they are fixed or mobile. The mobile enterprises, by definition, move their operations on more or less regular schedules among a number of different locations. Table 4.5 shows the specific categories of nonfarm activity which contain numbers of mobile enterprises. While some activities are not suited to enterprise mobility and have none or very few of the traveling entrepreneurs in their midst, others, such as vending of kitchen wares, herbal remedies, and used clothing, may have a third to more than three quarters of their number operating as mobile enterprises. Overall, 8.5 percent of all sampled enterprises were mobile (this does not include the operators of matatu taxis).

Slightly under half the interviewees lived on the premises in which the enterprise was carried on. Those living off the premises mostly lived within 3 miles of it. The propinquity between place of work and residence is related to the long hours that most people work: fewer than ten percent worked under 8 hours per day, three-quarters worked 8-12 hours, while the rest spent almost all their waking hours "on the job."

Physically, the premises appear to fall into two broad categories. The larger group--around three-quarters of the enterprises--are located in solid permanent structures with a concrete floor, concrete or stone walls, and a corrugated iron roof. In the smaller group which includes some mobile entrepreneurs such as clothing vendors and fruit and vegetable sellers, the "premises" are much less substantial. Usually, articles for sale are spread on the ground, but in some cases vendors have some sort of stall, perhaps with a roof for shelter. Only one enterprise in seven had running water, but one in three had electricity: by 1977, rural electrification had reached quite a substantial proportion of the sampled market centers in Central Province.

Among the mobile enterprises, the degree of mobility differed markedly with the type of activity practised but was generally low in comparison with those of West Africa and Asia. Only a handful of mobile entrepreneurs visited more than four market centers with any regularity, while fully 30 percent confined their selling activity to only two centers, and another 30 percent visited only three markets on a regular basis. Enterprises dealing in crafts, clothing, manufacturing, and services were the most mobile. Seventy-five percent of this group went to three or more different centers regularly. Farm produce vendors and herbalists traveled the least among mobile vendors: 57 percent of them frequented fewer than three markets on a regular basis. While distances traveled and

TABLE 4.5

SAMPLED MOBILE ENTERPRISES AND NONFARM ACTIVITIES

Nonfarm Activity Category	Number of Sampled Nonfarm Enterprises	Number of Mobile Enterprises	Mobile Enterprises as a Percentage of Nonfarm Enterprises	Percent Total Mobile Enterprises in Activity Category
Beverage making (pombe brewing)	17	1	5.9	1.4
Fiber-product making (e.g., weaving, basketry, rope making)	6	5	83.3	7.0
Wood-product making (e.g., furniture, handles, and carts)	34	3	8.8	4.2
Metal-product making (e.g., manufacture of farm, household and other implements)	19	3	15.8	4.2
Construction and building material production	4	2	50.0	2.8
Wholesale trading	5	1	20.0	1.4
Vending of new and used clothing	47	23	48.9	31.9
Catering (e.g., operators of food kiosks and meat roasters)	28	1	3.6	1.4
Other retailing (including farm produce, household utensils, snuff)	107	29	27.1	40.3
Herbalists and traditional healers	3	2	66.7	2.8
Other services	22	2	9.1	2.8
TOTAL	292	72	24.7	100.0[α]

SOURCE: Rural Nonfarm Survey of Central Province, 1977.

[α] Total does not add to 100% because of rounding.

numbers of different markets frequented were low, however, there was a notable pattern of repeat visits each week to one or more favored markets. Sixty-three percent of mobile entrepreneurs journeyed on two or more separate occasions per week to one favored market, while 20 percent made repeated visits to two or more centers. Once again, dealers in household utensils and clothing had the highest proportion of "full time" mobile entrepreneurs, because around 65 percent of each of these two groups was selling in some marketplace on four or more occasions each week. For the sample as a whole, however, the proportion of "full time" entrepreneurs was relatively low: almost 50 percent limited their visits to a market place to three days or less per week.[4]

Employment Characteristics

As we have seen, two-thirds of the enterprises are operated by the owner or his family without the assistance of salaried managers. Even so, it is difficult to detect clear differences in demographic characteristics between owners and salaried managers or assistants. In what follows they are grouped together as "nonfarm workers."

Previous Work Experience

Only 30 percent of the interviewed nonfarm workers claimed they were qualified for another job. The jobs most frequently mentioned were farming, tailoring, furniture making, construction, and business services. A variety of reasons were offered for not taking up these other occupations. Table 4.6, which lists them, shows that the difficulty of finding a vacancy, lack of capital, and

TABLE 4.6

REASONS FOR NOT TAKING UP ANOTHER OCCUPATION

		Percent (N=256)
1.	Cannot find a vacancy in that occupation	27.3
2.	Unable to raise the necessary capital	24.6
3.	The pay is less	23.4
4.	Family obligations	4.3
5.	Costs too much to move	1.6
6.	Other reasons	18.8
Total		100.0

SOURCE: Central Province Nonfarm Survey, 1977.

---

4. Donald B. Freeman, "Mobile Enterprises and Markets in Central Province, Kenya", *The Geographical Review* 70 (1980): 43-45.

the lower income in that occupation were roughly of equal
importance. It seems clear that operators of nonfarm activities are
not simply "marking time" while waiting for an opening in a
preferred formal sector job for which they are trained.

Table 4.7 provides evidence that points to a fairly high level
of employment mobility within the nonfarm sector. Half of the
interviewees had been previously employed in the same sector,
usually in a different occupation. Equally important, fully
one-third of the interviewees had previously been unemployed, an
indication of the level of unemployment in rural areas. The
remainder had either previously farmed a smallholding or had been a
student or an apprentice.

TABLE 4.7

PREVIOUS OCCUPATION OF THE INTERVIEWEE

	Percent (N=852)
Student or apprentice	8.6
Unemployed	31.2
Another job in the nonfarm sector	39.2
Same job in another enterprise	7.7
Farming	9.5
Other	3.8

SOURCE: Central Province Nonfarm Survey, 1977.

The strong neighborhood effect that was evident both in
location of residence and in the location of other enterprises in
which the interviewee was a part owner, is also to be found in the
location of previous occupations: table 4.8 shows that half of the
previous occupations were within ten miles. Even more interesting,
20 percent were previously employed in Nairobi, which suggests that
circular migration, as described by Elkan, is still occurring on a
substantial scale.[5] The main reason for leaving the previous
occupation appears to be a strong desire to raise income levels.
Immediately before joining the enterprise, the average net monthly
wage was KShs 153; immediately after, it was KShs 224, a rise of
nearly 50 percent.

---

5. W. Elkan, "Circular Migration and the Growth of Towns in East Africa,"
International Labour Review 96 (1967): 581-589.

TABLE 4.8

LOCATION OF PREVIOUS OCCUPATION

	Percent (N=500)
In the same location	38.2
Less than 10 miles away	9.4
More than 10 miles away	32.0
In Nairobi	20.4

SOURCE: Central Province Nonfarm Survey, 1977.

Education and Training of Nonfarm Workers

Great variations are evident in the interviewees' formal education. As table 4.9 shows, over seventeen percent had no formal education, while at the other extreme, over sixteen percent had ten or more years of formal education. The modal group had from six to eight years of education. Using the educational attainment of all heads of rural households in Central Province as a benchmark, we find that enterprise operators in market centers have achieved a much higher level of education on average. The differences are especially marked for the category with no education: nearly two-thirds of all rural household heads fall in this group, but only 17 percent of market center enterprise operators. Taking this further, a three way cross-tabulation of activity by sex by education reveals that the majority of operators who lacked any formal education were women operating fruit and vegetable stands. Aside from these people, there can be no doubt that most operators in the rural nonfarm sector in Central Province have had considerable exposure to formal education.

The rural nonfarm sector itself fulfills an important role in job training and raising the skills of the workforce. The number of true apprentices (56, working in 36 establishments) is not large but is still significant. More importantly, many of the 185 semi-skilled employees were upgrading their skills, with the intention of becoming skilled employees. Indeed 90 percent of paid employees were trained on the job, with the remainder being equally divided between being trained at schools or at rural Craft Training Centers, previously called Village Polytechnics.[6]

---

6. David Barker, "The Craft Training Center as a Rural Mobilization Policy in Kenya," *Rural Africana* 12-13 (Winter-Spring 1981-1982): 75-90.

TABLE 4.9

YEARS OF FORMAL EDUCATION: COMPARISON WITH HEADS OF
HOUSEHOLD, I.R.S. SURVEY OF CENTRAL PROVINCE

Highest Level reached	I.R.S. (Central Province)	Central Province Nonfarm Survey N=849
None	64.4	17.3
Standard 4	24.0	22.0
Standard 7 or 8	8.6	44.5
Form 2 and over	3.1	16.2
Total	100.0*	100.0

SOURCE: *Integrated Rural Survey 1974-75: Basic Report*, table 6.7, p. 36; Central Bureau of Statistics, Ministry of Finance and Planning; Central Province Nonfarm Survey, 1977.

Table 4.10 shows the proportion of nonfarm operators trained in educational institutions. There are some slight, but interesting, differences between the training of operators and of their employees. Over 92 percent of the owner/operators were trained "on the job," and only 7 out of 844 were trained at Craft Training Centers (CTCs). However, 5 percent of employees were trained at CTCs. This suggests that some students graduating from the CTCs are now finding jobs in the nonfarm sector, but have not yet risen to the level of manager or operator of the enterprise. Clearly, the rural nonfarm sector fulfills a very important role in teaching technical and entrepreneurial skills.

In summary, a comparison of levels of education of heads of all rural households in Central Province and of the enterprise operators reveals some startling differences in training and expertise of nonfarm operators. In the latter group five times as many have had formal education beyond Standard 6. Conversely in the province, 64.4 percent of all rural household heads have no formal education, as compared to only 17.3 percent in the nonfarm enterprises. It would appear that although the basic technical skills are acquired outside the formal school system, the broader skills of reading, writing, and numerical facility are acquired within it. Moreover, for nonfarm activities having higher labor productivity, there is strong evidence that enterprise operators combine informally acquired technical skills with formally acquired skills of literacy and numeracy.

TABLE 4.10

TRAINING OF OPERATOR CROSS-CLASSIFIED BY ACTIVITY
(PERCENTAGES)

Activity	School	Rural Craft Training Center (Village Polytechnic)	On the Job	Other
Primary Extraction and food industries	2.3	0.0	95.3	2.3
Textiles and clothing	4.7	1.2	91.8	2.4
Wood and Metal fabrication	18.2	7.3	72.7	1.8
Dukas	3.9	0.5	94.6	1.0
Hotels, bars and restaurants	1.9	0.0	97.2	0.9
Butchery and Meat Roasting	1.6	0.0	96.8	1.6
Other Vending	2.5	0.6	96.2	0.6
Petrol stations and repair shops	14.0	0.0	80.0	6.0
Other services	6.5	0.0	88.3	5.2
All Activities	5.0	0.8	92.3	1.9

SOURCE: Central Province Nonfarm Survey, 1977.

Prob < .0001

Some would argue that the increasing number of operators with
formal school qualifications mainly reflects rising expectations and
that these qualifications serve to exclude the peasantry from
entering such occupations, without being of any practical
significance in operating the enterprise. The evidence would seem
to contradict this interpretation. Most entrepreneurs need to be
able to keep basic accounts, to order and check inventory, and to
plan their cash flow. Literacy is equally important in reading
government reports, newspapers, and other sources of business
information and in writing letters, accounts, order forms, and
government forms. Thus one important group of business skills is
acquired within the formal school system. Being familiar with the
use of telephones is also important: recent research indicates that
a surprising amount of business information is transmitted by rural

telephone.[7] Finally, numeracy is important in order to keep a rudimentary balance sheet, in ordering inputs such as wood, cloth, and sheet metal, and in keeping a record of customer credit.

Technical Characteristics of the Enterprise: Labor Intensive and Adaptive Technology

Most enterprises have long, regular operating hours. Fully 36 percent close "hardly ever", and most of the remainder close only for public holidays. Only a third of the enterprises were closed on Sunday. Thus, although rural markets may be periodic, many market center enterprises operate continuously, some making goods on non-market days for sale when the market is in full operation.

Despite the fact that one-sixth of the assets of nonfarm enterprises were in the form of tools and equipment, simple to intermediate technologies were generally used. It goes without saying that there were big differences from activity to activity. This is reflected in the depreciated current assets per employee shown in table 4.11. Thus, nearly three-quarters of nonfarm workers

TABLE 4.11

DEPRECIATED CURRENT ASSETS PER EMPLOYEE: SELECTED ACTIVITIES

Activity	Depreciated Current Assets (KShs.)	Number of enterprises
Woodcutters	9	5
Wooden handle makers	83	2
Traditional healers	855	3
Food kiosks	3,852	28
Clothing vendors	5,304	47
Pombe brewers	8,248	17
Furniture makers	16,001	32
Dukas	20,235	208
Matatu (taxi) operators	21,415	10
Posho mills	23,424	11
Weighted arithmetic mean (all enterprises)	11,138	852

SOURCE: Central Province Nonfarm Survey, 1977.

---

7. D.D. Cleevely and G. Walsham, *Modelling the Role of Telecommunications within Regions of Kenya* (Department of Engineering, University of Cambridge, 1981). Mimeograph.

use hand tools, one-quarter--mainly clothing vendors and the like--do not. Ten percent use power tools, these being mainly activities in the manufacturing sector. Only 24 out of the 852 enterprises owned a motor vehicle; these were mainly matatu (taxi) operators and sawmills.

The technologies used by the informal sector are generally assumed to require smaller inputs of capital, but larger inputs of labor, than those used by the formal sector. Many studies, including Kenneth King's investigation of Kenya's informal sector, indicate that this is the case.[8]

In practice, two effects are at work. First, there is a compositional effect. The informal sector is engaged in a wide range of activities that are ignored by the formal sector, and vice versa. Thus the informal sector does not engage in the manufacture of petro-chemicals, nor the formal sector in the weaving of sisal baskets. These are activities where one mode of production has a clear advantage. The rural nonfarm component of the informal sector has a clear advantage in a wide range of activities that are difficult to mechanize, have short production runs (often custom work), and involve little commodity capital. Examples include: hunting, bamboo and wood cutting, charcoal making, sisal, reed and bead products, wooden handles, wood and stone carving, letter writing, and translating among numerous others.

The second effect involves activites that may be mechanized and thus in which similar products can be produced both by the formal and the informal sector. The formal sector, for example, refines oil, while the informal sector recycles used oil by filtering out larger particles in suspension; the formal sector makes shoes on mechanized production lines, while the informal sector hand-crafts shoes, often to order; the formal sector mass produces light bulbs, while informal producers make oil lamps out of recycled oil cans. As Bienefield suggests, the informal sector often occupies market niches that are too small to interest the formal sector.[9]

One particular aspect of informal activity is especially labor intensive, namely repairing. Third World societies assiduously recycle goods and materials. Whether it is repairing a vehicle or a bicycle, altering secondhand clothing or repairing a watch, a radio, or machinery, the capital inputs are usually limited to a spare

---

8. Kenneth King, *The African Artisan: Education and the Informal Sector in Kenya* (London: Heinemann, 1977).

9. M. Bienefield, "The Informal Sector and Peripheral Capitalism: The Case of Tanzania," *Bulletin of the Institute of Development Studies* 6 (1975): 53-73.

part, frequently locally made, and one or two specialized tools. Labor inputs, in contrast, are generally large. Table 4.12 gives details of capital and labor inputs for several repairing activities, and compares them to the informal manufacturing

TABLE 4.12

CAPITAL AND LABOR INPUTS FOR SELECTED MANUFACTURING
AND REPAIRING ACTIVITIES

	Frequency	Employees per Establishment	Assets (KShs.)	
			per estab.	per employee
Manufacturing Activity				
Posho Milling	11	1.5	48,312	23,424
Pombe Brewing	17	4.5	64,095	8,248
Tailoring	57	1.4	10,010	7,044
Sawmilling	2	13.5	265,000	19,630
Furniture Making	32	2.4	38,501	16,001
Blacksmithing	16	1.6	7,950	4,988
Repairs				
Footwear Repairs	10	1.5	3,826	2,551
Clothing Repairs	5	1.0	1,039	1,039
Car Repairs	8	4.6	12,144	2,626
Bicycle Repairs	18	1.1	3,555	3,199
Tool and Machinery Repairs	1	1.0	400	400
Miscellaneous Repairs	14	1.3	5,345	4,157

SOURCE: Central Province Nonfarm Enterprise Survey, 1977.

sector.[10] The overall impression gained from the Central Province
Survey is of a sector characterized by labor-intensive production
functions. But it must be stressed that this average masks very
considerable variability.

"Informal" Technical Training

The term "informal" was originally used to describe an
unregulated trading and production system. It has since been
applied to a much wider range of activities, including informal
housing, informal health care, and informal education. Most of the
skills acquired by practitioners in the informal sector were
acquired within an informal system of education, and not in formal
schools.[11] This is shown to be broadly true for Central Province
(table 4.10), but there is one important caveat. Informal education
begins at a young age. Outside school hours, nearly every "fundi"
(artisan) is watched by youngsters who closely observe his craft.
In due course, these youngsters "graduate" to become unskilled
assistants, often on a part-time basis. In turn, some rise to
become true apprentices (in the sense that they pay an apprentice
fee), but many more become poorly paid assistants with the low wage
reflecting a hidden apprentice fee. Eventually, the survivors
become fully paid employees, or, if they have access to the
necessary capital, they set up their own enterprise.

Consistent with the argument that on-the-job training
predominates is the finding that more than seventy percent of the
interviewees were not qualified to do another job. Of the
remainder, the biggest group had skills as farmers while a handful
had skills in various manufacturing, repairing, and service
occupations which were usually acquired on the job.

The average enterprise had tools (excluding vehicles) valued
at KShs 3,300, which is a substantial investment. Since there are
certain disadvantages to an enterprise holding large liquid assets,
we inquired whether there were any tools that were owned but not
used: nearly 8 percent of the respondents replied in the
affirmative and on average valued these tools at KShs 1,455. This
is circumstantial evidence in support of the argument that some
entrepreneurs over-invest in tools in order to remain deliberately

---

10. William House draws similar conclusions from a study of Nairobi's
informal sector. See W.J. House, "Nairobi's Informal Sector: An Exploratory
Study," in *Papers on the Kenyan Economy: Performance, Problems and Policies,* ed.
Tony Killick (Nairobi: Heinemann, 1981), pp. 357-368.

11. International Labour Office, *Employment, Incomes and Equality: A
Strategy for Increasing Productive Employment in Kenya* (Geneva: International
Labour Office, 1972).

illiquid.[12] Besides substantial investments in tools and equipment,
143 enterprises also rented tools, nearly always from private owners
(as opposed to rental companies). The average monthly payment for
the tools and equipment rented was close to KShs 80.

The informal sector has, in summary, been identified in many
studies as the primary user of intermediate technology. The
extensive use of hand tools and the more limited adoption of power
tools, electricity, and motor vehicles are indicative of this. It
should not be assumed, however, that tools and equipment are
unimportant. Typically, they form a quite substantial proportion of
the enterprise's assets, in addition to the widespread practice of
renting tools.

Economics of the Nonfarm Enterprise
Initial Capital

The average amount of the initial investment in an enterprise
made by the interviewee was KShs 3,872. In 9 out of 10 cases, the
main source of capital for investment was personal savings, with
loans from relatives as a secondary source (5.5 percent).
Government loan schemes through the Industrial and Commercial
Development Corporation (ICDC), the District Joint Loan Boards, and
the Kenya National Trading Corporation (KNTC) played an
insignificant role in the establishment of new small enterprises in
rural areas of Central Province. Commercial banks and private
moneylenders were likewise unimportant as a source of investment
capital.

As tables 4.11 and 4.12 suggest, the initial capital needed to
start an enterprise varied considerably from activity to activity.
It is evident, for example, that there are quite a number of
activities for which the capital costs of entry are minimal. For
wood cutting, charcoal making, and a number of craft industries the
capital inputs were often less than KShs 100. The income and
profits to be earned from these activities, however, were
correspondingly small. By contrast, the average capital investment
required to establish an enterprise in Central Province was KShs
3,950 or about US $500, which is equivalent to over a year's income
for the average head of household. Moreover this average hides a
distribution skewed towards higher values (the standard deviation
was KShs 11,819). For the more lucrative occupations, entry costs
exceed KShs 20,000 ($2,500) which is, in the context of local income

---

12 . Thorne Walden, "Entrepreneurial Illiquidity Preference and the African
Extended Family," in *Development Planning in Kenya,* ed. Tom Pinfold and Glen
Norcliffe, Atkinson College Geographical Monograph no. 9 (Toronto: York
University, 1980), pp. 119-140.

levels, a very large figure. Capital can be raised on this scale
only through such avenues as using a title to a *shamba* (farm) as
security for a bank loan or obtaining a loan from wealthy relatives.
Having a well-paid job in the formal or informal sector or receiving
a windfall are other ways of raising investment capital. In
practice, nearly 90 percent of the entrepreneurs used personal
savings to establish an enterprise.

Once established, it seems that enterprises in the rural
nonfarm sector were generally profitable and expanding. When asked
about changes in sales since the time of establishment of an
enterprise, the ratio of those reporting an increase to those
reporting a decrease was 3:1 with only 14 percent reporting no
change. The main reasons given for a decline in sales were
competition from other enterprises and rising costs. For expanding
firms, the main causes cited were an increase in local demand
(possibly attributable to the coffee boom, then at its height) and
becoming better known in the community.

Given the generally healthy picture that emerges, it might be
asked why more establishments were not opened. However, 80 percent
of the establishments reported difficulties in getting started,
which suggests that there are certain barriers to entry in this
sector. As table 4.13 shows, the biggest problem is raising the
cash to establish the enterprise. The only other common problem is
finding and holding a market for the goods or services.

Interviewees were asked to estimate the original investment
and the current value of the investment in the main categories shown
in table 4.14. This table, reporting the average amount in each
category, needs interpreting carefully. For instance, frequency of
response differed among the categories; the time lapsed since
initial establishment differs; the initial investments are not
expressed as current values; and, for long-established enterprises,
the interviewees' recollections were probably imprecise.
Nevertheless the magnitudes between initial and present values are
so large that the data clearly indicate a rapid rate of capital
accumulation. Bearing in mind that the median enterprise had
operated for a 3-year period during which inflation rates had been
fairly low, we can conclude with some confidence that the capital
invested in an average enterprise had increased roughly threefold
since its establishment.

TABLE 4.13

PROBLEMS IN STARTING AN ENTERPRISE

	Percent (N=670)
Raising the capital	76.6
Finding suitable premises	19.4
Finding suitable enployees	4.6
Finding a good location	5.2
Obtaining a license	8.1
Obtaining raw materials or inputs	19.6
Selling the product or services	35.2
Others	17.3

SOURCE: Central Province Nonfarm Survey, 1977.

TABLE 4.14

AVERAGE INITIAL CAPITAL INVESTMENT AND PRESENT
VALUE OF CAPITAL INVESTED IN MAJOR CATEGORIES

	Initial Investment KShs.	N	Current Value KShs.	N
Land	71	686	1,515	810
Buildings	800	694	8,113	818
Tools and equipment	771	688	3,305	828
Stocks of materials and products	1,891	693	5,405	833
Vehicles	644	698	1,990	838
Advance rent on buildings and equipment	325	698	–	–
Other	252	697	23	839
Total (unweighted)	4,754		20,351	

SOURCE: Central Province Nonfarm Survey, 1977.

Present Capital Structure

Two major elements in the capital structure of an enterprise are the site and the premises in which it is located. Table 4.15 indicates that the great majority of enterprises rented both the land and the premises: only 13 percent owned the land, while slightly more--19 percent--owned the premises. In some instances, such as fruit and vegetable sellers, the "premises" were very simple structures. This is consistent with the picture that we have presented earlier: the availability of premises for rent removes one conceivable barrier to entry and encourages a fair degree of mobility in and out of business.

TABLE 4.15

OWNERSHIP OF LAND AND PREMISES

	Land		Premises	
	No.	%	No.	%
Rented	712	87.0	662	81.1
Owned	106	13.0	154	18.9
Total	818	100.0	816	100.0

SOURCE: Central Province Nonfarm Survey, 1977.

The current depreciated value of enterprises in each activity category is given in *Appendix II* (table 1). The mean of KShs 19,772 conceals a range from KShs 9 for woodcutters to KShs 265,000 for sawmills. Interviewees were asked to break down the total assets of an enterprise into the components shown in table 4.16. Land and buildings account for a little under half of the total assets, even though over 80 percent of the enterprises rent them. For the 89 establishments that own both the land and buildings the average value was KShs 65,024, while for the 39 who own the premises only, the average value was KShs 57,439. Such an amount--close to US $8,000--would be a formidable barrier to entry if most firms were not able to rent premises. Stocks account for a quarter of the capital assets, while tools and equipment are also quite important.

When asked if the enterprise made a profit, 15 percent replied "No," another 15 percent did not know, and the remaining 70 percent replied in the affirmative. For the enterprises making a profit, the average monthly amount (after deducting wages, living expenses,

TABLE 4.16

PERCENTAGE BREAKDOWN OF CURRENT ASSETS FOR THE AVERAGE ENTERPRISE
(AVERAGE TOTAL ASSETS: KShs. 19,772)

	Percent (N=833)
Value of land	7.4
Value of buildings	39.9
Value of tools	16.2
Value of stocks	26.6
Value of vehicles	9.8
Value of other items	0.1
Total	100.0

SOURCE: Central Province Nonfarm Survey, 1977.

etc.) was KShs 576. Half of the profits were re-invested in the
same enterprise, which is consistent with the historical growth of
assets discussed in the previous section. A quarter was spent on
consumption and a further 15 percent were saved.

A similar impression is also gained from the question: "Are
you expanding this enterprise at the moment?" A positive response
was given in 20 percent of the interviews. In most cases the
expansion was to occur at the present site, but in one out of five
cases the expansion was to be located somewhere else. For 162
enterprises, the average cost of the expansion was KShs 20,850 which
again points to quite rapid capital accumulation and expansion. The
major source of capital for expansion was personal savings and
re-invested profits. Importantly, in 25 percent of the cases, the
entrepreneur identified ICDC or KNTC as the major potential source
of capital. Thus it appears that these parastatals are more likely
to make loans to help established and viable enterprises to expand,
than to finance the creation of new enterprises with an uncertain
future. Typically the expansion would create two or three new jobs,
and in two-thirds of the cases the range of products or services was
to increase.

Inputs to the Enterprise

The scale of operation of nonfarm enterprises is small by most
measures. The mean value of monthly inputs was KShs 5,165 (about US
$700). A breakdown of these inputs for various nonfarm activity
groups is given in table 4.17. As shown, wholesale manufactured or

TABLE 4.17

MONTHLY COST OF INPUTS PER ENTERPRISE

Activity Group		Salary and Wages	Raw Materials	Wholesale Goods	Transport	Water	Electricity	Other	Total
1. Primary extrac- tion and food industries	KShs. %	864 13.3	4340 67.0	475 7.3	536 8.3	15 0.2	150 2.3	98 1.5	6478 100.0
2. Textiles and clothing	KShs. %	313 21.5	405 27.8	693 47.6	28 1.9	10 0.7	4 0.3	4 0.3	1357 100.0
3. Wood and metal fabrication	KShs. %	734 16.8	1258 28.7	1040 46.6	290 6.6	5 0.1	45 1.0	6 0.1	4378 100.0
4. Dukas	KShs. %	336 5.4	257 4.1	5422 86.7	203 3.2	18 0.3	14 0.2	2 0.0	6252 100.0
5. Hotels, bars and restaurants	KShs. %	677 13.3	485 9.5	3713 72.9	119 2.3	69 1.4	26 0.5	7 0.2	5096 100.0
6. Butchers and meat roasters	KShs. %	310 9.1	1657 48.4	1360 39.7	50 1.5	39 1.1	7 0.2	1 0.0	3424 100.0
7. Other vending	KShs. %	305 6.5	694 14.9	3478 74.6	172 3.7	5 0.1	7 0.1	0 0.0	4661 100.0
8. Petrol stations and repair shops	KShs. %	823 8.3	879 8.9	8056 81.6	51 0.5	16 0.2	41 0.4	3 0.0	9869 100.0

101

		460	181	230	15	3	8	80	977
9. Other services	KShs. %	47.1	18.5	23.5	1.5	0.3	0.8	8.2	100.0
ALL ACTIVITIES	KShs. %	463 9.6	786 16.3	3361 69.7	155 3.2	20 0.4	23 0.5	14 0.3	4822 100.0

SOURCE: Central Province Nonfarm Survey, 1977.

processed goods accounted for almost 70 percent, raw materials for
16 percent, labor costs nearly 10 percent, transport 3 percent, and
other items such as water and electricity under one percent.

Sources of Inputs

The average monthly cost of inputs from wholesalers (who in
turn make purchases from the formal sector) is to some extent the
result of including a wide range of retailing activities, including
petrol stations, as part of the rural nonfarm sector. But even
manufacturing activities make substantial purchases from the formal
sector: this is true, for example, of tailors who are (numerically)
the single largest manufacturing activity. Indeed there is only one
activity group--the primary extraction and food processing category
accounting for only 5 percent of the sample--in which indigenous raw
materials predominate over inputs from wholesalers. Overall, less
than one-fifth of the costs of inputs for the rural nonfarm sector
are accounted for by indigenous raw materials. The pattern is
somewhat different, however, for actual purchase or acquisition of
inputs. On average, nearly 40 percent of physical inputs came from
the local area (within 5 miles). Another 28 percent came from
Nairobi, most of the remainder coming from wholesalers in major
towns who are, in turn, supplied from Nairobi. Thus locally
acquired inputs, mainly from farms and resource extraction
operations, are of considerable importance, but are somewhat smaller
than inputs coming directly and indirectly from Nairobi. The main
form of transportation used to deliver inputs is vehicles not owned
by the enterprise: this includes trucks owned by wholesale companies
and soda and beer manufacturers, matatu taxis, and country buses.
Another 14 percent was delivered by human carriers, the commodities
involved being mainly farm and other resource products.

Wages and Incomes

Details of the cost of inputs for the 9 major activity groups
given in table 4.17 show that labor costs for nonfarm enterprises
are proportionately highest in the "other services" group, followed
by the various manufacturing activities. They are lowest for dukas
(partly because of the large input of unpaid family help).

In manufacturing, wage levels paid to employees varied
somewhat but were generally low. A few skilled employees earned as
much as KShs 800 per month, but the median was close to KShs 200 per
month (about US $25). Wage levels for semi-skilled employees were
only slightly less, which is not surprising in a labor surplus
economy. The average wage for apprentices was KShs 87 per month.
These figures compare with an average wage in formal manufacturing
of KShs 597 in 1977.

Details of household income and expenditure for the interviewees themselves (who were mostly owner operators) need interpreting with care. Many variables are subject to seasonal variations, particularly those relating to income from, and expenditure on, a shamba. Some interviewees found it difficult to separate their business accounts from their household accounts. Also, the raw data suggest that average household expenditure somewhat exceeds household income. Many households did, however, receive goods and services in kind from the business enterprise, particularly those owning food kiosks, hotels, dukas, clothing stores, and the like.

Bearing in mind these difficulties, the following broad picture emerges. The average wage paid to the operator in Central Province was KShs 260 per month. For many households, this was not the only source of income. Other sources included payment in kind from the enterprise, remittances received from relatives (this mainly applies to people in the lower income group), income in cash and kind from the smallholding, income earned by other household members, and income from other enterprises. Although the questionnaire did not solicit complete information on household income, judging from partial information and patterns of expenditure, we estimate average *household* monthly income to be close to KShs 500, spent as follows: food and clothing, KShs 330; school fees, KShs 55; remittances to relatives, KShs 85; and other expenses, KShs 30.

Other Costs and Inputs

An important operating cost is rent paid for the land and/or premises. The average monthly rent was KShs 150 for both land and premises. For the 8 percent of entrepreneurs who owned their premises but rented the land on which they were situated, the average monthly rent was KShs 104.

Nonfarm enterprises also make fairly substantial payments to the Government. The largest of such outlays was for license fees, averaging KShs 270 per year. Taxes averaged KShs 34 per year, and other payments KShs 39. In total, the 836 enterprises responding to this question paid KShs 287,000 to the public sector in 1976. To put this figure in perspective, the *annual* amount paid to the Government is a little less than the *monthly* wage bill for the same enterprises.

Sales and Credit

The average value of monthly sales was KShs 5,400. Since only one-third of the enterprises close on Sunday, this implied daily sales of around KShs 200 (US $25) which is quite small. With this level of inputs and sales, it is not surprising that few entrepreneurs were able to purchase their own premises or expensive equipment. Out of the average monthly sales recorded by the enterprises sampled, around 88 percent was sold for cash and the remaining 12 percent for credit. Barter sales were uncommon. On the whole, credit sales were more common in larger enterprises such as sawmills; small enterprises extend very little credit and many operate strictly on a cash payment system. Consequently the average credit owing to an enterprise--KShs 555--though not insignificant, is less than the average monthly sales made on credit. Presumably debts are paid off quite quickly.

Three-quarters of the enterprises reported seasonal fluctuations in their sales level, the remaining one-quarter describing sales as being uniform throughout the year. The main cause of seasonality is the cycle of planting, cultivation, and harvesting on small farms. Sales are higher after the harvest when cash crops are sold. A second peak in sales is recorded on holidays, particularly at Christmas. Sales were reported to be highest in the months from August to December.

188 businesses (mainly manufacturers) reported stocks of raw materials, ranging in value from a few shillings to as high as KShs 40,000 with an average of around KShs 1,300. The average stock of products for sale was KShs 5,068 which is quite substantial.

Competitiveness of Enterprises

Reference has been made earlier to the competitive nature of the rural nonfarm sector. The average interviewee claimed that there were around 8 effective competitors in his or her line of business, over three-quarters of these being in the same sub-location. To be sure, the presence in most market centers of Central Province of many small enterprises often performing similar functions strongly suggests that the rural nonfarm sector is highly competitive. Indeed, for activities with minimal barriers to entry, the situation appears to come close to perfect competition. In practice, this picture needs qualifying in two respects. The sector is not entirely unregulated. And for activities with substantial barriers to entry, the market is much less than perfectly competitive.

The basic regulation on enterprise operators is that they must obtain a license. These are fairly easy to obtain, although 5

percent of the interviewees reported difficulties in becoming
licensed. There is also a handful of unlicensed enterprises
(including some barbers), but they are unimportant. License fees
usually cost from KShs 50 to KShs 200 which is not intimidatingly
large although the license for a bar generally exceeded KShs 1,000.
But there are more subtle controls. For instance, successful
bicycle repairers often wish to progress to assembling new bicycles
by obtaining an ICDC loan. But loans from DJLBs and ICDC are highly
competitive: only a few entrepreneurs obtain this official sanction
in their efforts to grow.

Table 4.18 records the number of local competitors in the same
line of business as the interviewees, disaggregated for the main
activity groups. There is much variability, but, overall, retailing
appears to be more competitive than manufacturing and repairing. In
primary extraction, wood and metal fabrication, petrol stations, and
repair shops, there are rarely more than 3 or 4 competitors and
frequently less.

These data are only indicative, because it is difficult to
present firm evidence on the competitiveness of markets. The
existence of considerable barriers to entry and the size of profits
reported in some enterprises lead one to suspect that in some market
centers and in some activities competition is somewhat imperfect.
It may be self evident that as the number of competitors increased,
competition was increasingly reported as a problem for the
entrepreneur. But the reverse interpretation is more illuminating:
the 15 percent of enterprises with no competitors and the 25 percent
with only one competitor clearly benefitted from that situation.

Economic Linkages of Nonfarm Enterprises

Nonfarm enterprises are embedded in a web of linkages that
bind them into the rural economy and at the same time fit them in a
peripheral fashion into the national and international economic
systems. The pattern of local enterprise linkages includes those
within the rural nonfarm sector itself, comprising sub-contracting
and capital transfers among jointly owned enterprises or those of
clansmen or neighbors.

Almost 10 percent of the interviewees were owners or
part-owners of other nonfarm enterprises, three-quarters of these
being located less than ten miles away. Coupled with the fact that
nearly 10 percent of the enterprises were owned by partnerships,
this suggests that entrepreneurship is flourishing but is subject to
a strong neighborhood effect so that business ventures are only
rarely located far from their home base. The mean income for the
previous year for those with an interest in one of these other

106

TABLE 4.18

NUMBER OF COMPETITORS REPORTED BY ENTREPRENEURS FOR MAJOR ACTIVITY GROUPS

Number of Competitors	Primary	Textiles & Clothing	Wood & Metal	Dukas	Hotels	Butchery	Other Vendors	Petrol Stations	Other Services	All Activities
0	25.0	12.0	34.5	2.0	6.5	24.2	17.0	32.7	21.3	15.0
1-2	22.7	37.3	36.4	5.6	27.8	30.6	13.1	38.8	41.3	23.1
3-5	31.8	26.5	18.2	14.7	39.8	24.2	20.3	20.4	21.3	23.0
6-10	6.8	19.3	7.3	27.9	20.4	14.5	16.3	6.1	2.7	16.8
11-20	2.3	4.8	3.6	36.0	2.8	4.8	21.6	0.0	4.0	14.5
20+	11.4	0.0	0.0	13.7	2.8	1.6	11.6	2.0	9.3	7.5

SOURCE: Central Province Nonfarm Survey, 1977.

nonfarm enterprises was KShs 3,322, which averages KShs 277 a month, a not inconsiderable amount in local terms.

Interestingly, only 21 out of the 852 enterprises belonged to a cooperative society. There is, nevertheless, considerable interdependency amongst the firms; 76 out of 841 enterprises subcontracted. Moreover, 80 percent of this subcontracting occurred within the same sub-location, which suggests a high level of informal co-operation amongst neighboring enterprises and the generation of significant multiplier effects in employment. The importance of subcontracting is even greater when it is considered on a sectoral basis. It is not practiced to any significant degree in retailing and services. One-third of the enterprises in the wood and metal fabrication group, nonetheless, subcontract work. For the 76 enterprises that subcontract, the average payment for work contracted out was KShs 330 per month. This is not an insubstantial amount, suggesting that, at least at the time the interviews were conducted, the sector was economically buoyant.

The linkages outside of the nonfarm sector, however, represent an indication of the significance of the nonfarm enterprise as a factor in the whole process of rural development. These linkages include those with small scale agriculture, with resource exploitation as exemplified by the Kenyan forest industries and with large scale urban enterprises whether these be in the parastatal sector, the urban private sector (especially wholesalers) or the urban informal sector. The above case study outlining the operation of the nonfarm enterprise in Central Province sets the stage for analysis of these linkages with other sectors of the economy. Once again we use data on Kenya as a whole supported by information collected in the Central Province Survey. These linkages form the subject of the following two chapters.

CHAPTER V

RELATIONS BETWEEN THE RURAL NONFARM SECTOR AND RESOURCE EXTRACTION AND AGRICULTURAL SECTORS

Although the relations between the nonfarm sector and other economic sectors are of considerable importance to an understanding of the development process, they have not received much attention to date. As a result, little is known about these intersectoral linkages. The lumping together of urban informal and nonfarm sectors in most previous studies had served to cloud these relationships further. Where such linkages have been mentioned, it is often assumed that they are weakly developed.[1] New evidence, however, suggests that the rural nonfarm sector is not at all isolated from other sectors. We deal with some of this evidence in this chapter. In particular, we examine relationships of the rural nonfarm sector with two other rural sectors, the resource extraction sector (forestry is selected as a detailed example), and small-scale agriculture.

Nonfarm Relations with Resource Extraction Activities

As one would expect, biotic resource industries are located mostly in areas of Kenya that are better favored climatically, where rainfall exceeds 400 millimeters per year and growing conditions are suitable for forestry as well as agriculture. Because there are few commercially viable mineral deposits in Kenya and wild game trophies have been banned since 1977, the resource extraction sector is dominated by forestry and fishing activities. Fishing is regionally important around Lake Nyanza, Lake Turkana, and along the Indian Ocean shore. Elsewhere it is either absent or negligible. Total Kenyan production of fish in 1978 was valued at K£ 4.3 million.[2] Forest industries, however, are more widespread, and some sort of wood products are produced even in remote, semi-arid areas of the country. Furthermore, the forest products industry has a sizeable

---

1. For example, see Judith Heyer, Dunstan Ireri, and Jon Moris, *Rural Development in Kenya* (Nairobi: East African Publishing House, 1971), pp. 113-114.

2. Republic of Kenya, Central Bureau of Statistics, *Statistical Abstract 1979* (Nairobi: Government Printer, 1979), p. 135.

110

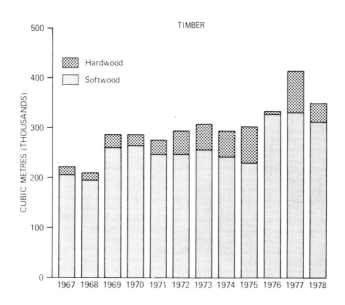

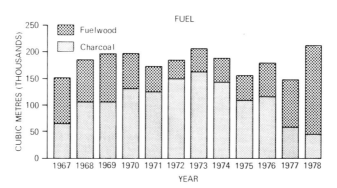

Source: Republic of Kenya, Ministry of Economic Planning and Community Affairs, Economic Survey, 1980 (Nairobi: Government Printer, 1980), p. 134.

Fig. 5.1   Growth in demand for Kenyan forest products

111

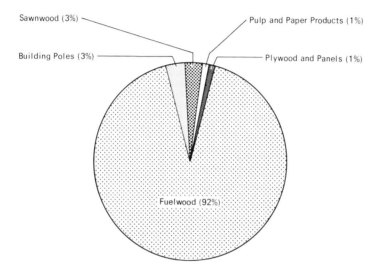

Source: Forest Department, Kenya Ministry of Natural Resources, 1974

Fig. 5.2 Consumption of forest products by product category

small-scale component as well as a large-scale, urban milling and
fabricating component. Small-scale activities include charcoal
making and selling, basic sawmilling and wood working, and craft
industries such as carving, making tool handles, and furniture.

Charcoal Making

Charcoal is an almost universal heating and cooking fuel in
Kenya and is usually produced by small operators working in the
forests or in the bushland. The activities of charcoal burners are
widespread in rural Kenya, where larger trees and even acacia thorn
scrub are cut and slowly burned to produce rough charcoal that is
bagged and sold to dealers by the roadside. The dealers transport
the charcoal to market centers and towns, where major concentrations
of consumers are located. As figures 5.1 and 5.2 show, the use of
timber for fuel, both in the form of charcoal and firewood, is
overwhelmingly the main component of Kenya's forest industries.
According to the IRS nonfarm module (see table 3.7) the number of
specialist charcoal producers is relatively small indicating that
this activity is most commonly a part-time venture for rural
dwellers, supplementing incomes from farming or other activities.
Monthly incomes from charcoal selling are modest, averaging KShs 206
per month (see table 3.13).

Sawmilling

Few of the sawmills operating in Kenya are large. A survey of
58 licensed sawmills in all forest conservancies conducted in 1974
revealed that most had an annual output of less than 3,000 cubic
meters of sawn timber. The market for this output, which is given
in figure 5.3, indicates the importance of non-monetary and
intermediate consumption. The location of sawmills is shown in
figure 5.4. Many of the larger mills are located in or near to the
main urban centers of Kenya, while the majority of small mills are
in the forests themselves or in rural market towns. Some, but not
all, of these small mills are informal sector enterprises. Many are
located along the western scarps and slopes of the Great Rift
Valley, as well as the forested uplands of Kiambu District, the
Aberdare Range, and Mount Kenya.

A study of the sawmilling industry in the mid-1970s revealed
that the small rural mills differed from their larger urban
counterparts in a number of important respects.[3] The small,
forest-located mills had a high proportion of their employees

3. Donald B. Freeman and Birger Solberg, "Effects of Mill Location, Size,
and Input Characteristics on the Economic Efficiency of Kenya's Forest
Industries," *Tijdschrift voor Economische en Sociale Geografie* 69 (1978): 141-153.

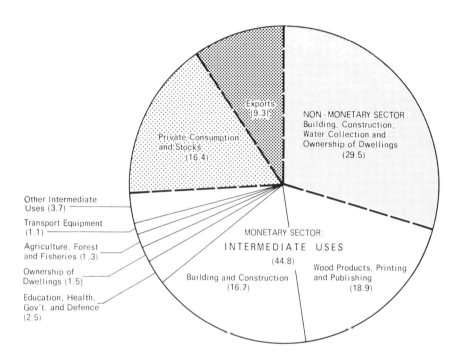

Exports
(9.3)

Private Consumption
and Stocks
(16.4)

NON - MONETARY SECTOR:
Building, Construction,
Water Collection and
Ownership of Dwellings
(29.5)

Other Intermediate
Uses (3.7)

Transport Equipment
(1.1)

Agriculture, Forest
and Fisheries (1.3)

Ownership of
Dwellings (1.5)

Education, Health,
Gov't. and Defence
(2.5)

MONETARY SECTOR:
INTERMEDIATE USES
(44.8)

Building and Construction
(16.7)

Wood Products, Printing
and Publishing
(18.9)

TOTAL: £ (Kenyan) 3,474,000

Source: Republic of Kenya, Ministry of Finance and Planning.
Input - Output Table for Kenya, 1967.
Nairobi: Government Printer, 1972.

Fig. 5.3   Percentage utilization of forestry output by
economic sector

114

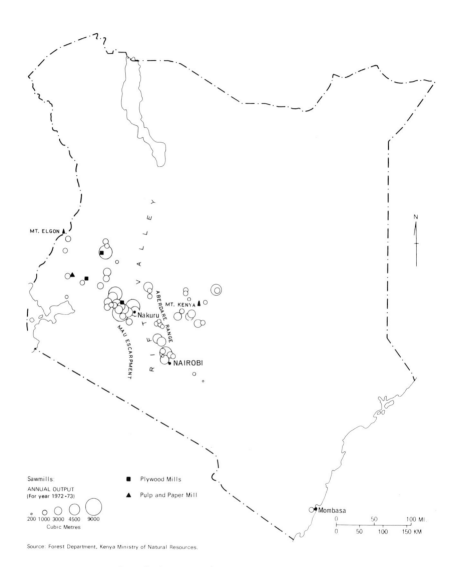

Fig. 5.4 Location of Kenyan sawmills

engaged in actual logging operations. Urban mills, in contrast, had a high proportion of labor in skilled occupations such as processing and fabricating, joinery, and prefabricated house production. The level of capitalization was different: small-to-medium sized mills have highest value-added per employee (figure 5.5), but the forest-located mills are often under-capitalized, with adverse effects of outdated equipment being felt via a generally low quality of output. Rural consumers accept this lower-quality output: the demand level for sawn timber of better quality in rural areas is not high. For the high-quality urban market, small rural mills send much of their output by rail to the larger urban mills in the form of rough-squared timber for further processing. Thus, as far as their market area is concerned, the mainly small, basic rural sawmills--without equipment for producing sophisticated joinery products--have local sales, or else are "tied" to one or more large urban mills as suppliers of rough-squared timber. The small sawmills in the rural nonfarm sector thus act as suppliers of cheap construction material in areas where sawn-timber for houses or commercial buildings is in demand (the larger rural towns and market centers in the more prosperous farming regions of Kenya, primarily).

Incomes and employment for basic sawmilling are highly variable. This variability is related to the degree of capitalization, the value of timber type used--camphor and mvule are more valuable than exotic softwoods and cedar--the depletion of available stands of timber near to the mill, the plantation softwood timber available, and the nature and purchasing power of the market for sawn timber. As a component of the rural nonfarm sector, therefore, small sawmills show a high degree of dependency on the urban sector for markets and some inputs and seem unlikely to expand independently.

Other Resource Industries

Of minor significance in the array of resource industries are other activities such as gatherers and makers of animal and vegetable fiber products and water sellers. Even before the government ban on hunting wild game in 1977, there were relatively few legitimate African hunters licensed in rural areas of Kenya, since this was still a preserve of white settlers and large urban-based safari companies. But some small producers of domestic animal hides and skins have continued to operate in rural Kenya, as the data from the IRS and Central Province Surveys show. Since the standard of tanning of skins is uneven, these are not exported in

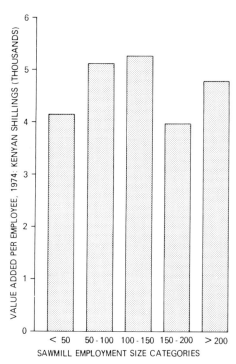

Source: Forest Department, Kenya Ministry of Natural Resources.

Fig. 5.5 Value added per employee in Kenyan sawmills by mill size category

quantity from the local production area, but mostly supply the needs
of the rural residents, with some sales to the informal sector in
Nairobi.

Nonfarm Relations with Agriculture

By far the most significant set of relationships among rural
subsectors are those between the nonfarm sector and small-scale
agriculture. If we arbitrarily define two elements in both sectors,
namely a household and an enterprise, then four major relationships
can be identified:

1. Relationships in which agroprocessing industries convert farm
   products and sell them to or through some type of marketing
   organization
2. Relationships involving the provison by nonfarm enterprises
   of productive inputs for farmers, including tools,
   fertilizer, and seeds
3. The provision, through nonfarm activities, of various
   household needs of farmers, who pay for these by off-farm
   sales of produce; and
4. Movement of labor and capital between farm and nonfarm
   production units in harmony with the seasonal rhythms of
   agriculture.

Agroprocessing and Produce Marketing

Only a few products from Kenya's small farms are "exported" in
their original state: considerable value is added to farm products
by the nonfarm sector. Coffee is processed from freshly picked
berries to dried beans; grain and sugar are milled; sisal and
pyrethrum are processed; cattle are butchered for meat, and their
hides, horns, and hooves are fashioned into a variety of useful
products. Fruit and vegetables are dried, frozen, canned, and made
into preserves and beverages. Thus the rural nonfarm sector does
much more than merely trade farm produce. In many instances a
considerable amount of processing occurs, often on the same farms
where the produce is grown.

In addition, a variety of nonfarm activities in the rural
markets are directly related to farming. In the Central Province
Survey, these activities comprised over 20 percent of the complete
sample. Some enterprises surveyed contributed value-added to farm
produce by processing food or raw materials or making beverages
(table 5.1). These include butchers, *posho* (maize meal) millers,
pombe (traditional beer) brewers, producers of fiber products and
leather, and tobacco and snuff makers. In some cases, the

manufacture and retailing of these products are carried out by the same entrepreneurs, making simple categorization impossible. Certain categories of food and raw material processing, however, are absent from the list of activities found in rural markets, instead coming under the jurisdiction of national processing and marketing boards. All maize and other grains not destined for local consumption, for instance, come under the purview of the Maize and Produce Boards.

Farm Input Suppliers

The rural nonfarm sector also plays an important role in providing farm inputs. In Kenya, organizations such as the Kenya Farmers Association (KFA) are major suppliers of seeds, feed, and fertilizer, but small scale enterprises do play a part, especially by manufacturing and repairing tools and equipment, and providing transportation and storage of produce.

Table 5.2 shows the relative importance of nonfarm enterprises which supply material and service inputs to agriculture in Central Province, Kenya. For example, producers of metal farm implements and vendors of hardware and farm supplies (over 2.0 percent of total respondents) comprise a small but significant group of nonfarm activities directly providing productive factor inputs to agriculture. Frequently these enterprises employ locally produced inputs themselves and apply "appropriate" technology. Cost savings and convenience to farmers provided by local repair services and agricultural produce storage are vital to the maintenance of agricultural productivity.

Rural Household Needs

As we have shown in chapter 3, local enterprises provide for many needs of rural households, particularly of farms that are partly or completely commercialized, and of households that are engaged in nonfarm production. These locally provided goods and services are often in direct competition with imported goods from overseas or from factories in Nairobi. Household needs cover a wide range of products, such as those discussed in chapter 3, but also include a great variety of services. Rural residents evidently purchase many needed items from local nonfarm enterprises, as opposed to purely subsistence sources or suppliers in towns. It is clear from evidence presented earlier that the nonfarm activities in market centers play a vital role in the provision of goods and services, particularly to the rural poor. Only in the case of items such as furniture, which are normally comparison goods rather than

TABLE 5.1

NONFARM ENTERPRISES ENGAGED IN AGROPROCESSING AND
MARKETING OF FARM PRODUCE

N = 852

Enterprise Type	Percent of Total Sample in Central Province
Maize (posho) Milling	1.29
Dairy Products	0.23
Pombe (Beer) Brewing	2.82
Other Beverages and Tobacco Products (incl. Snuff)	1.52
Fiber Products	0.23
Animal Skins and Leather Products	3.52
Butchery and Meat Products	4.34
Vegetable and Fruit Marketing	5.05
TOTAL	19.00

SOURCE: Central Province Rural Nonfarm Enterprise Survey, 1977.

TABLE 5.2

NONFARM ENTERPRISES PROVIDING DIRECT INPUTS TO
AGRICULTURE (GOODS AND SERVICES)

N = 852

Enterprise Type	Percent of Total Central Province Sample
Metal Farm Implement Manufacture	0.23
Hardware/Farm Supplies	1.99
Repair and Servicing of Machinery and Automobiles	5.52
Storage of Agricultural Produce	0.12
TOTAL	7.86

SOURCE: Central Province Rural Nonfarm Enterprise Survey, 1977.

convenience goods, do the majority of rural consumers patronize
enterprises located in towns in preference to other sources of these
goods.

Needs of the Rural Nonfarm Sector

Further evidence of the important ties between the small farm
sector and rural nonfarm activities is given in table 5.3, which
lists the main sources of supply of all major classes of nonfarm
activities and is based on the 1977 Central Province Survey of
Nonfarm Enterprises. As shown in this table, a number of nonfarm
activities rely on purely local sources of inputs (or else sources
less than five miles distant). These include not only manufacturers
of wood products and meat products, but also enterprises engaged in
wholesaling and retailing, including restaurants, bars and hotels,
food kiosks, and herbalists. In contrast, most dukas drew the bulk
of their inputs from beyond five miles, and over 18 percent stated
that the majority of their inputs came from the city of Nairobi. Of
all the categories of activity investigated, Nairobi appears as a
source of inputs for nonfarm enterprises in 19.7 percent of cases,
and non-local sources (beyond five miles) account for a further 32.6
percent of cases. Clearly, for some nonfarm activities, urban
suppliers exert a strong effect which is spreading the influence of
external capital into the rural economies of Central Province.
Firms requiring manufactured inputs, such as those engaged in
automobile repair, drew inputs from urban suppliers. In general,
agroprocessing activities have the most highly developed local
backward linkages, while other activities are to a greater or lesser
extent linked into interregional and urban supply channels.

Sales by Nonfarm Enterprises

Patterns of sales by enterprises in Central Province directly
dealing in farm produce are shown in table 5.4. Clearly, it is not
only the categories engaged in agroprocessing and farm produce
collection, bulking, and distribution that have overwhelmingly local
sales: this applies in all categories. Fully 72.3 percent of the
sampled respondents stated that the bulk of their sales were to
customers in the same sub-location. Categories such as butchers,
food kiosks, meat roasters, dukas, bars, restaurants and hotels, and
food and raw material processing all had over 80 percent of
respondents reporting concentrations of local sales. Very few
enterprises in any category concentrated on selling to customers
outside the local area or to Nairobi. Within the larger picture of
spatial trade linkages, it is clear that rural economies of Central

Province are largely localized, but there is also a one-way flow of
interregional trade in manufactured goods from Nairobi and other
urban centers into the small rural centers. There is minimal supply
of goods other than farm produce in the reverse direction via the
rural markets where the majority of small nonfarm entrepreneurs are
clustered. National marketing boards which can control agricultural
product prices seem to be the main channels for interregional flows
of farm goods, not small scale enterprises in local free markets.
This appears to signify that local markets, although important, are
not playing to the full the role envisaged for them by growth-pole
theorists, who see them as gateways for the beneficial two-way flow
of goods through the urban hierarchy to rural dwellers. There is,
therefore, some evidence of a net outflow from rural areas to
Nairobi of cash--rural savings and surplus--constituting a potential
backwash of rural capital. The implications of this pattern are
explored below.

Flows of Capital and Labor

In view of the fact that many owners or operators of nonfarm
enterprises also own (or share ownership of) small farms, the
potential for flows of capital and labor between nonfarm and small
farm sectors is considerable. Data from the Central Province Survey
show that nonfarm activities do provide some funds for investment
in, or operation of, farms but that the amounts are smaller than
might be anticipated. More than half of the respondents who owned a
shamba (small farm) and who admitted receiving some farm income,
spent a portion of the proceeds from their nonfarm enterprise on
inputs or improvements to their farm in the month preceding the
survey. Indeed, eleven percent of those with incomes from a farm
spent large amounts (more than KShs 500 or US $66) on their farm in
the previous month. Surprisingly, about 15 percent of the landless
group contributed money to the running of a *shamba* in the previous
month. This presumably represents investment in a relative's farm.

The data led to the conclusion that nonfarm activities in
Central Province at the time of the survey did not provide much
direct investment or operating capital for the farms owned by
nonfarm entrepreneurs. But cash flows in the opposite direction
appear to be substantial, i.e., farms owned by nonfarm entrepreneurs
appear to be a significant source of investment capital for
enterprises in the rural nonfarm sector. This tends to support
findings in an earlier, more general study by Jennifer Sharpley.[4]

---

4. Jennifer Sharpley, "Resource Transfers between the Agricultural and
Non-Agricultural Sectors: 1964-1977," in *Papers on the Kenyan Economy:
Performance, Problems and Policies* (Nairobi: Heinemann, 1981), pp. 311-319.

TABLE 5.3

SOURCES OF INPUTS INTO RURAL NONFARM ENTERPRISES

(Percentages of Central Province enterprises in major nonfarm categories having over two-thirds
by value of their inputs drawn from suppliers in particular distance categories)

Sample Size = 356

Nonfarm Activity	Locations of Supply Sources				
	(Percent of sampled enterprises in each major category)				
	Same Location	Within 5 miles excl. same locn.	Over 5 miles excl. Nairobi	Nairobi	Geographically diverse sources
1. Raw Material Extraction, Food and Beverages, Fiber Products, Construction	33.3	14.3	38.1	0.0	14.3
2. Textiles, Clothing, Leather	29.4	0.0	38.2	24.2	8.2
3. Manufacture of Wooden and Metal Goods	43.8	6.3	25.0	12.5	12.4
4. Dukas (General Retailing)	17.5	6.2	41.2	18.4	16.7
5. Bars, Restaurants and Hotels	47.8	6.5	23.9	6.5	15.3
6. Butchers, Food Kiosks, Meat Roasters	41.7	16.7	16.7	0.0	24.9

7. Specialized Wholesale and Retail Selling, including Mobile Vendors of Clothing and Utensils	16.0	2.0	44.0	32.0	6.0
8. Automobile and Machinery Repairs and Services	9.1	4.5	13.6	68.2	4.6
9. Transport, Community and Personal Services	34.5	10.3	13.8	17.2	24.2
TOTAL	27.0	6.5	32.6	19.7	14.3

SOURCE: Central Province Nonfarm Survey 1977.

NOTE: Row figures may not add exactly to 100% due to rounding.

TABLE 5.4

LOCATIONS OF MAIN CONSUMERS OF NONFARM GOODS AND SERVICES

(Percentages of Central Province enterprises in major nonfarm categories having over two-thirds
by value of their sales made to customers in particular distance categories)

Sample Size = 357

Nonfarm Activity	Location of predominant body of consumers				
	(Percent of sampled enterprises in each major category)				
	Same Location	Within 5 miles excl. same locn.	Over 5 miles excl. Nairobi	Nairobi	Geographically diverse sources
1. Raw Material Extraction, Food and Beverages, Fiber Products, Construction	81.0	0.0	4.8	0.0	14.2
2. Textiles, Clothing, Leather	52.9	5.9	2.9	8.8	29.5
3. Manufacture of Wooden and Metal Goods	43.8	0.0	0.0	0.0	56.2
4. Dukas (General Retailing)	83.3	4.4	0.9	0.0	11.4
5. Bars, Restaurants and Hotels	82.6	4.3	0.0	2.2	10.9
6. Butchers, Food Kiosks, Meat Roasters	88.0	0.0	0.0	4.0	8.0

7. Specialized Whole-sale and Retail Selling, including Mobile Vendors of Clothing and Utensils	52.0	4.0	4.0	0.0	40.0
8. Automobile and Machinery Repairs and Services	68.2	0.0	9.1	0.0	22.7
9. Transport, Community and Personal Services	69.0	3.4	3.4	0.0	24.2
TOTAL	72.3	3.4	2.2	1.4	20.7

SOURCE: Central Province Nonfarm Survey, 1977.

NOTE: Row figures may not add exactly to 100% due to rounding.

When amounts of initial investment in nonfarm activities are categorized, it is apparent that nonfarm entrepreneurs who were also *shamba* owners were able to begin operations with higher capitalization than were the subsistence and landless groups. Almost 23 percent of farm owners were able to put an initial investment of KShs 5,000 (US $666) or more into their nonfarm enterprise, while less than 12 percent of the subsistence and landless entrepreneurs were able to amass that level of initial investment. The difference in the patterns of investment by the two groups was found to be statistically significant at the 1 percent level.

This difference is reinforced when data on present capitalization of nonfarm enterprises are examined. Shamba owners are, once again, more numerous in the higher categories (over KShs 10,000 or US $1,333). The difference in patterns of present capitalization between the two groups is in this case also statistically significant at the one percent level. The two groups naturally differed in the proportion of nonfarm profits spent on farms. The mean for group one (commercial small-farm owners) was 4.9 percent of reported profits, while for subsistence and landless entrepreneurs, the mean was virtually zero. As regards capitalization of nonfarm activities, farm owners have become preponderant in the more highly capitalized forms of enterprise, like dukas.

This comment is underscored by data on present market value of businesses. In 1977, the mean value for enterprises owned by the first group of respondents--those with farm income--was KShs 27,689 or US $3,692, while the mean for the second group of respondents--subsistence farmers and landless--was KShs 14,530 or US $1,937. Thus, again it appears that the flow of capital between the farm and rural nonfarm sectors is not balanced but that the nonfarm sector is supported in a fairly substantial manner by capital infusion from the small farm sector, at least in certain categories of activity such as duka operation.

Supplementing farm income is another way in which the agricultural and nonfarm activities are linked functionally. Although 42 percent of the respondents owned a *shamba*, 73.4 percent of the complete sample consumed their entire month's earnings from the nonfarm enterprise without spending any money on farm operation. Clearly, for many farm families, the operation of the nonfarm activity is viewed as a simple means of supplementing income from the farm or (if a subsistence smallholding) providing needed cash for goods not obtainable from the farm itself. A certain proportion of many entrepreneurs' earnings was remitted to families, usually living on near-subsistence farms, and in this way, rural incomes are further supplemented. There was no significant difference, however, in the amount remitted between the two groups distinguished above (farm owners and landless).

The factor of seasonality has bearing on relations between farm and nonfarm enterprise operations. Almost 75 percent of respondents recorded marked seasonality of nonfarm activity sales. As indicated earlier, the greatest number (45 percent) of respondents mentioned harvest time as having a strong influence on the pattern of sales, while the second most frequently stated influence was the spending increase around Christmas and other festivals (28 percent of respondents). The effect of harvest periods could mean several different things in the case of part-time farmers who own or manage nonfarm enterprises. Their own harvests may bolster their nonfarm enterprise through purchases of more inventory than usual with harvest proceeds. Also, the general level of spending in the local rural community probably increases at such times. Conversely, farm owners may be forced to spend more time attending to their harvests and less time running the nonfarm enterprise, and thus the increase in sales may be less than potentially realizable. Christmas and other holidays, when gifts are given or when festivals take place, normally stimulate such nonfarm activities as sale of clothing, which tend to attract higher proportions of landless entrepreneurs. In general, however, it seems that the important linkage of cash transactions between farm and nonfarm sectors is subject to fluctuations that largely originate in the seasonal rhythm so characteristic of farming.

The interchange of labor between nonfarm and small-farm sectors is no less significant than flows of capital. The factors affecting labor apportionment in the case of joint ownership of farms and nonfarm enterprises are complex. Apart from the seasonal cycle in agriculture mentioned above which frees labor at certain times of the year for nonfarm employment, these influential factors include: the division of labor in the rural household which sees men, particularly younger ones, frequently dominating cash-generating nonfarm activities and many women acting as managers on behalf of their husbands; the scale of operation; and the commercial or subsistence orientation of small-farm operations.

Thus, of the nonfarm entrepreneurs in the Central Province Survey who owned farms, 79.2 percent were male. It was discovered that males dominate nonfarm activities whether or not farm ownership is involved, but their dominance is more pronounced where their farm has a cash income. Among respondents who had a cash farm income, males represented 80.4 percent, whereas among the respondents without a cash income from their farms or who were landless, males represented 72.9 percent. Shambas with incomes have relatively fewer females participating in nonfarm activities than shambas without incomes or where a family does not own a farm. The distinction between patterns of farm income/lack of income and sex of nonfarm respondents in the Central Province Survey proved to be statistically significant at the five percent level. This suggests that nonfarm activities are neither the exclusive province of a class of successful farmers branching out into other fields, nor the preserve of farmer's wives deriving a secondary income from sale of produce and cottage crafts. Although some of both classes of entrepreneur are present, the predominance of males with low farm incomes or without farms altogether indicates that market enterprises in Central Province are the principal bread-and-butter activities of the majority of participants.

The ages of rural residents appear to have a bearing on the probability of their contributing to flows of cash or labor between nonfarm and small farm sectors. Analysis of survey data relating to age revealed that over three-quarters of respondents under 40 years of age have no farm income, whereas over 42 percent of respondents aged 40 years or more had a cash income from a farm. The proportion of those who are landless or have only a subsistence farm rises to 86.5 percent among respondents in the 20-30 year age group. The emerging landless class in rural Central Province, not unexpectedly, is a new generation. Those in the more fortunate position of having both farm and nonfarm income, and for whom the issues of farm-nonfarm capital transfer and income supplementation have direct relevance, are an aging group. Of the group without a farm income, a higher proportion are relatively well educated. 54.6 percent of this group have at least three years of schooling, as against 39.9 percent in the group who have a farm income. Again, the distinction in educational patterns between farm owners with farm income and those without farms or farm income was statistically significant at the 1 percent level.

Effect of Farm Ownership on Nonfarm-Small Farm Linkages

There are significant differences in patterns of participation in particular categories of nonfarm activity between farm owners and landless entrepreneurs (table 5.5). In the case of markets in Central Province, the proportion of farmers who are duka (retail store) owners or managers is almost double that of landless entrepreneurs. The reverse is true for wholesale/retail selling of clothing, household utensils, and other goods. Relatively more farm owners were involved in extractive and food processing activities than were landless individuals. More landless persons, nonetheless, were involved in operation of food kiosks or butcheries, and in wood and metal product manufacture.

There appears to be no significant difference between wage levels paid to employees in enterprises operated by farm owners and those operated by landless people. However, there are significant differences in the patterns of capital/labor and capital/output ratios as regards farm-owners and landless peasants. Farm owners tend to be relatively more numerous in the higher categories of both of these ratios. For the former ratio, the mean value for the farm-owner group was 64.43, as against 36.36 for the landless group. The difference proved to be statistically significant based on Student's t test. The conclusion suggested by these data is that activities operated by part-time farmers are both more highly capitalized and less efficient than those run by landless entrepreneurs, for whom the activity is likely to be the sole means of earning an income. There were no significant differences between the two groups as regards numbers of employees or hours of unpaid family help obtained by respondents in operating their businesses. The average nonfarm enterprise in Central Province employs about 0.7 workers. While each individual enterprise is very small, the vast numbers of these rural enterprises make them a potentially large source of (admittedly low-paying) wage employment for the country as a whole.

There are appreciable differences in wages among individual nonfarm activity categories. For example, wages in food and fiber products processing (category 1 in table 5.3) appear relatively low (mostly below KShs 500 or US $66 per month). Similar wage patterns are observable for unskilled jobs such as butchers, kiosk operators, and meat roasters, and for the category of vendors and sellers other than dukas. In contrast, more skilled jobs, as in wooden and metal goods manufacture, show a much higher proportion of well-paid employees (nearly a third receive above KShs 500 or US $66 per

TABLE 5.5

COMPARISON OF NONFARM ENTERPRISE TYPES
INVOLVING (A) OWNERS OF COMMERCIAL FARMS AND
(B) SUBSISTENCE FARMERS AND LANDLESS PEOPLE
(Sample Size = 852)

Nonfarm Activity	Commercial Farm Owners* (Percent)	Subsistence Farmers and Landless People (Percent)
1. Raw Material Extraction, Food and Beverages, Fiber Products, Construction	5.9	4.7
2. Textiles, Clothing, Leather	9.5	10.3
3. Manufacture of Wooden and Metal Goods	4.5	7.9
4. Dukas (General Retailing)	31.8	19.0
5. Bars, Restaurants and Hotels	12.8	13.0
6. Butchers, Food Kiosks, Meat Roasters	7.0	7.5
7. Specialized Wholesale and Retail Selling, incl. Mobile Vendors of Clothing and Utensils	14.0	22.3
8. Automobile and Machinery Repairs and Service	6.1	5.7
9. Transport, Community and Personal Services	8.4	9.7

NOTE: Column totals may not add exactly to 100% due to rounding.

*Those reporting a cash income from their Shamba (small farm) when interviewed in 1977 Central Province Nonfarm Survey.

month), and almost a fifth are paid over KShs 1,000 (or US $133 per month). In short, the main activities that employ rural labor, most of it probably drawn from local farms, are low-paying. Wage employment as a means of supplementing farm income seems not as attractive an alternative, however, as more rewarding but riskier self-employment in rural or urban small business.

Nonfarm activities, it is clear, often yield higher marginal returns than simply increasing the effort and time spent in crop cultivation. Of course, for the younger generation, there is often no alternative to nonfarm wage labor or self-employment (or migration to Nairobi). Out of the total sample, about ten percent, however, gave farming as their previous occupation before engaging in their present nonfarm activity. This indicates a significant permanent switch of labor from small farm to nonfarm sectors.

The evidence presented above indicates that both the dispersed sphere and the concentrated (marketplace) sphere of nonfarm activities have important functional linkages with small-farming in Central Province. In both cases, nonfarm activities provide income supplements, enable part-time farmers to fill the seasonal hiatus more productively between planting and harvesting and are mutually supportive of farming in terms of capital flows and the provision of needed goods and services. These relations have a bearing on longer-term rural development processes and on development policy.

Mutual Development Relationships of Farm and Nonfarm Sectors

The basic development relationship between farming and rural nonfarm activity is their interconnected role in raising rural productivity and incomes. Some nonfarm activities use raw materials from farms, diversify the products available in rural areas by processing them in a variety of ways, and contribute value-added to farm products. They provide needed commercial outlets for rural produce, although as the evidence indicates, this "gateway" role is not functioning in the optimal fashion as envisaged by certain development theorists. Market center activities also provide inputs for farms which help to raise rural productivity, often with local materials and appropriate technology, although the dominance of Nairobi in the distribution of goods and services cannot be overlooked. Incomes of farms are raised directly by supplementary employment in various nonfarm activities that provide opportunities for earning incomes impossible to acquire if the farming sector dealt directly with the formal urban sector. Farm family incomes are also bolstered by remittances from relatives working elsewhere

including those in rural nonfarm activities. In turn, certain
nonfarm activities give rise to ancillary activities in the local
markets which provide additional job opportunities and incomes
through a system of multiplier effects. These local multipliers are
an important aspect of rural development, since they contribute to
rural employment and income. They also provide basic human needs,
except where they are overwhelmed by the strong effects of formal
activities in the dominant urban centers such as Nairobi.

This competition between rural nonfarm activities and their
urban counterparts has considerable bearing on rural development.
So long as rural enterprises can continue to compete successfully,
jobs will be available in the rural areas which pay well enough to
prevent many landless or under-employed rural residents from
migrating to the large cities. Insofar as local medium and high
value-added activities are involved, capital is generated and
retained in rural areas, and a measure of regional self-sufficiency
is achieved, fostered by the local complementarities of farm and
nonfarm activities. The creation of indigenous rural capital may
have the effect of forestalling dependency on non-local and overseas
capital which has been identified by many writers as a factor
hindering genuine development in rural areas of the Third World.

The considerable degree to which some market center activities
have already become linked into a national urban-distributive
system, however, means that numerous nonfarm enterprises have become
competitive with other rural activities, acting as channels for
extending the hegemony of large-scale urban manufacturers over rural
markets. By distributing urban manufactured goods which compete
with cottage crafts and small indigenous manufactures, some
enterprises in market centers may be viewed as detrimental to rural
development. This is because they may cause closure of small, local
manufacturing enterprises, may increase unemployment, might reduce
supplementary income in farm families that formerly relied on the
now-displaced manufacturing activities, and may have negative
multiplier effects on other rural activities. Evidence in this
study concerning the imbalance in interregional cash and commodity
flows through rural markets suggest that some of the deleterious
effects mentioned above may be operating in Kenya. The consequences
of this process are likely to be an increased reliance on urban
suppliers of goods, accelerating decline of small rural markets,
elimination of the dispersed type of nonfarm activity altogether, as
well as increased specialization and full commercialization of
small-scale agriculture. Evidence from a previous study indicates

that there have been strong shifts into specialized production of
cash crops in parts of Kenya's Central Province.[5] Thus, increased
dependency on urban manufacturers and specialized distribution
agents appears to be already well advanced in this part of Kenya.

In this context, a reminder about the atypical nature of
Central Province as regards dispersed nonfarm activities is timely.
Other areas of Kenya, such as Nyanza and Coast provinces, appear to
have far greater diversification of nonfarm activities, especially
in the more traditional categories. These "peripheral" provinces
seem also to be less well advanced than Central Province in shifting
to specialized commercial crop production. Consequently, they may
have a greater chance in the future of preserving a measure of
regional economic autonomy.

The purely local nature of agroprocessing activities in
markets of Central Province, in terms both of backward (input
supply) and forward (market) linkages has a bearing on the various
strategies for regional development discussed in chapter 1. Both
Richardson[6] and Friedmann and Douglass[7] have suggested that the best
strategy for genuine rural development is to create agroprocessing
industries in rural areas as a basis for generating outside income
and decentralizing high value-added production. The evidence from
this study, however, is that most agroprocessing activities
currently found in rural areas of Central Province are not basic
industries: they generate almost no cash income from outside the
local area in which processing takes place. An exception, of
course, is the existing activity of the various national marketing
boards dealing with such export crops as coffee and tea. But the
crops concerned are largely controlled by quotas set from Nairobi,
and the possibility for introducing new commercial crops that would
provide incomes for peasants without causing massive displacement of
marginal and subsistence producers remains to be demonstrated.

At the more general level of flows between agricultural and
non-agricultural sectors for the whole of Kenya, it is significant
that there has been a chronic net outflow of capital from
agriculture between 1964 and (at the latest available information)
1977.[8] This outflow consistently increased throughout that period

5. J. Tait Davis, op. cit., pp. 43-53.

6. Harry Richardson, op. cit.

7. John Friedmann and M. Douglass, "Regional Planning and Development: The
Agropolitan Approach," in *Growth Pole Strategy and Regional Development Planning
in Asia* (Nagoya: United Nations Center for Regional Development, 1976), pp.
333-387.

8. Jennifer Sharpley, op. cit.

and was a very high proportion of total gross fixed capital
formation in the agricultural sector. Sharpley makes the intriguing
comment that:

> Limited opportunities for on-farm investment have encouraged farmers to
> invest part of the funds from their net agricultural surplus in rural
> non-agricultural activities where the rate of return is higher . . . The
> largely voluntary nature of the net capital outflow is a logical
> response to market forces. High rates of savings and limited
> opportunities for profitable investment are consistent with low private
> rates of return on agricultural investment. The limited range of
> consumer items available in most rural markets contributes to the high
> savings rates, whilst profitable investment opportunities in the
> agricultural sector are limited by: the difficulty of buying small
> pieces of extra land; the lack of timely agricultural inputs at
> competitive prices from local dukas and marketplaces; and high costs of
> marketing, storing, and distribution which substantially reduce
> farm-gate receipts . . . many farmers find it more profitable and
> convenient to invest directly in non-agricultural activities rather than
> lend their agricultural surplus to financial institutions, who offer
> only 5 percent interest on savings deposits and do not actively solicit
> small depositors.[9]

These remarks are quite consistent with findings in the present
study.

---

9 . Ibid., pp. 317-18.

CHAPTER VI

RELATIONS OF THE RURAL NONFARM SECTOR WITH URBAN FORMAL, INFORMAL, AND PUBLIC SECTORS

In addition to the manifold interconnections between agriculture and the nonfarm sector, there also exist important connections with other major sectors. Certain subdivisions within the rural nonfarm sector receive a major proportion of their inputs from modern sector factories, and the relationship is strong enough to be classed as a form of dependency. For many other sub-sectors, however, nonfarm activities display a healthy degree of independence from the influence of the modern sectors. This chapter is centrally concerned with the nonfarm sector's relations with the urban formal sector. However, it also examines relations with the urban informal sector and with the public sector (comprising both government and parastatal agencies). But first we must set the stage by considering the general pattern of urban demand for rural products in Kenya.

Patterns of Urban Demand

A survey of urban purchasing patterns conducted by the Central Bureau of Statistics in 1977[1] summarizes the demand for rural products in Kenyan cities and towns. A sample of 471 urban households in all major urban areas was selected and monthly incomes and expenditures were recorded to identify patterns of demand. 81 percent of the urban households had only one income earner. Patterns of income and expenditure in the four major urban centers is given in table 6.1. Over 40 percent of average urban household expenditure was on food, with slight variations from town to town. In Nairobi and Mombasa, average food expenditures were over KShs 400 per month,[2] although households with incomes less than KShs 700 per month generally spent less. In accordance with Engel's Law, the very lowest income groups spent almost all (and in some cases, apparently more than) their revealed income on food. The main types

---

1. Republic of Kenya, Central Bureau of Statistics, "Urban Purchasing Patterns," *Social Perspectives* 3 (1978).

2. Ibid., table 23.

TABLE 6.1

KENYA: URBAN INCOME AND EXPENDITURE

(Percent of Urban Households)

City	Income (KShs. per Month)*						Expenditure (KShs. per Month)					
	<300	300-699	700-1399	1400+	Total	Mean	<300	300-699	700-1399	1400+	Total	Mean
	%	%	%	%	%	KShs.	%	%	%	%	%	KShs.
Nairobi	6.8	41.0	32.1	20.1	100	989	4.7	24.8	43.6	26.9	100	1182
Mombasa	5.8	49.2	24.2	20.8	100	1007	17.5	32.5	29.2	20.8	100	896
Nakuru	10.0	53.3	21.7	15.0	100	799	10.0	48.3	26.7	15.0	100	838
Kisumu	1.8	59.7	26.3	12.2	100	896	--	80.7	10.5	8.8	100	710
Total	6.4	46.9	28.0	18.7	100	958	8.1	36.5	33.8	21.6	100	1008

SOURCE: Republic of Kenya, Central Bureau of Statistics, "Urban Purchasing Patterns," *Social Perspectives*, 3, no. 1 (February 1978), tables 4 and 5, p. 6.

*Excluding households with incomes over KShs. 2,500.

of food purchased were cereals (mostly maize), meat, and milk, which collectively accounted for more than half the expenditure on food. Pre-packaged foods--evidence of urban processing--were hardly ever bought, save for a small fraction of the sample. Most food purchases were made at a retail shop rather than at a kiosk, market stall, or vendor (i.e., mostly from the formal sector rather than the informal urban sector). But it is highly probable that much of this food, on its way from the farmer's gate to the urban consumer's table, passed through the channel of the rural nonfarm sector and the produce-bulking dealer.

Hazlewood produces comparable figures on the proportion of urban consumer budgets spent on food. He says:

> In the budget used for computing the urban low-income price index, 70 percent of all expenditure on goods goes on food, drink and tobacco: the remaining 30 percent is spent on services--rent, transport, and education. About half the expenditure on food is on manufactured products, mostly maize meal and wheat flour, but also bread, sugar and cooking fat. Clothing and footwear take 15 percent, and fuel a further 6 percent. There is not much left for anything but a limited range of other manufactures. This budget relates to households with incomes of up to KShs 700 a month or K£420 a year. The pattern is not greatly different in the budget for middle incomes of between K£420 and K£1499. Food, drink, and tobacco, clothing and fuel together account for 87 percent of expenditure on goods, although the range of consumption of manufactured food is considerably wider than in the low-income group, and the amount spent is much greater. For incomes above K£1500 a year the proportion of expenditure on services is much higher, approaching one-half of all expenditure, because of high expenditures on rent and transport.3

Relations of the Nonfarm Sector with the Urban Formal Sector

The main sets of linkages between the nonfarm sector and the urban formal sector include: (1) relations of rural produce vendors and agroprocessors with urban produce-bulking dealers or factory processors; (2) purchase of goods by rural dukas or vendors from urban wholesalers and manufacturers and the related dependence of rural artisans and petty manufacturers on urban sources of input materials, tools, equipment, and technology; (3) the effects of extended family ties, including circularity in rural-urban migration streams and its influence on rural purchases by returning migrants as well as remittances by temporary urban workers to their rural kinfolk; (4) investments in rural enterprises by urban businessmen (and civil servants acting as businessmen), as well as by banks, and the reverse flows from nonfarm enterprises to urban investments; (5) competitive relationships involving inroads by large-scale and transnational enterprises into rural markets formerly supplied by rural nonfarm enterprises. These will be discussed in turn.

---

3. Arthur Hazlewood, op. cit., pp. 82-83.

Relations with Urban Produce Dealers and Processors

Table 6.2, which records the locations of customers of nonfarm enterprises, shows that only a small proportion of sales of nonfarm enterprises are made directly to urban areas such as Nairobi. But a vast amount of rural produce to which value has been added by agroprocessors in the nonfarm sector finds its way to urban consumers, through the activities of urban and rural wholesalers or produce bulkers, cooperatives, and governmental marketing agencies. Maize, for example, reaches the urban consumer in the form of sifted maizemeal produced in urban mills, after passing through the marketing and grading apparatus of the semi-governmental Maize and Produce Board. Vegetables and fruit, however, are marketed through less strictly regulated channels, being collected in rural marketplaces by private dealers who purchase truckloads of produce and transport these to the urban wholesale markets, from whence they are distributed to retailers. Generally a series of middlemen handle the produce between the farm and final customer. It is in the nature of produce bulkers and urban wholesalers that there are relatively few of them compared to the myriad urban retailers of produce, but the importance of the wholesale function is out of

TABLE 6.2

SOURCE OF PHYSICAL INPUTS AND LOCATION OF SALES

Source Area	Percentage	
	Inputs	Sales
Same sub-location	29.8	76.3
Within 5 miles	8.1	13.8
More than 5 miles	34.1	8.2
Nairobi	28.0	1.7
Total	100.0	100.0

SOURCE: Central Province Nonfarm Enterprise Survey, 1977.

proportion to the number of operatives engaged in it.

Note also the case of small sawmills which sell output to large, sophisticated urban mills that reap the benefit of higher capitalization. This is clearly an area in which undercapitalization and poor organization of small rural producers

permits large urban competitors to gain a major share of the
national and export markets to the detriment of the rural nonfarm
sector.

Demand in the urban informal sector is exceedingly difficult
to measure, and since it accounts for a major component of urban
consumption, it exacerbates the task of estimating aggregate urban
demand for specific goods and services--particularly the
intermediate demand. Estimates of aggregate urban demand for
products of the rural nonfarm sector are even harder to make,
although these are possible for some specific product groups. One
group for which a measure is available is the pattern of urban
demand for forest products, obtained in the survey of sawmill output
conducted in 1972-73 by the Ministry of Natural Resources. The
resultant pattern (figure 6.1) includes both formal sector and urban
informal demand for timber and other sawmill products. Not
surprisingly, the metropolitan area of Nairobi-Thika emerges as
overwhelmingly the most important market for commercial timber among
Kenya's urban centers.

An additional perspective on the formal sector market for
Kenyan forest products is given in figure 6.2. This shows that
wattle bark extract (used for tanning leather) far exceeds sawn
timber as the major export earner in the forest products sector.
Cowen has shown that wattle bark production in Kenya has been mainly
in the hands of the middle peasantry since the early 1940s.[4] The
wattle bark extract industry is thus one of the most basic of all
small-scale rural sectors. Given that much of the timber, wattle
bark, and allied rural nonfarm products are produced on land
unsuited for crops (water catchments, steep slopes, or semi-arid
areas), there is probably some capacity for expansion in this
sector; this would benefit peasant operators of small woodlots, or
those licensed to practice selective cutting of national or county
council forests.

Reliance on Urban Input Suppliers by Rural Vendors and Artisans

The primary sources of the goods sold in rural dukas and by
other small market vendors are urban manufacturers and importers.
This is indicative of a degree of urban dominance and rural
dependence. In the Central Province Survey, for example, it was
found that most dukas listed suppliers in Nairobi as their main
source of merchandise, accounting for a total of 87 percent of their

---

4. Michael Cowen, "Commodity Production in Kenya's Central Province," in
Rural Development in Tropical Africa, ed. J. Heyer, P. Roberts, and G. Williams
(London: Macmillan, 1981), pp. 121-142.

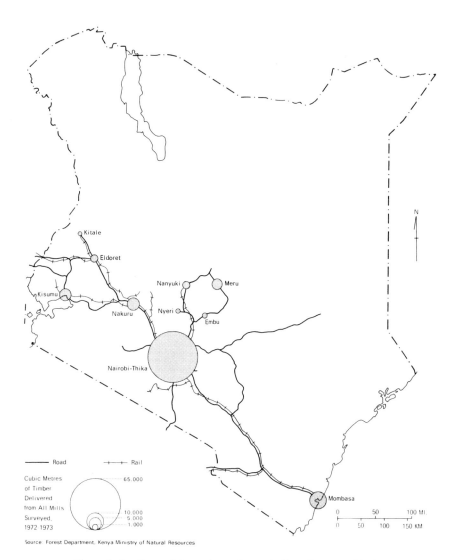

Fig. 6.1   Domestic urban demand for Kenyan timber

141

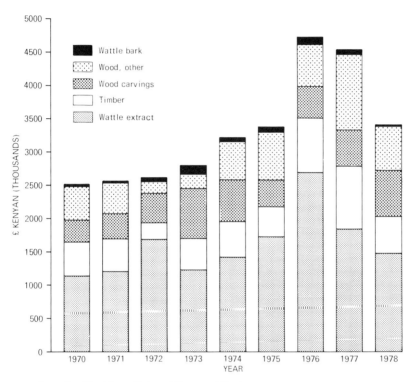

Source: Republic of Kenya, Ministry of Finance and Planning, *Statistical Abstract, 1973* (Nairobi: Government Printer, 1973), p. 683.

Fig. 6.2 Growth in exports of Kenyan forest products

inputs (by value). This dependence is particularly true for certain classes of rural vendors of products such as kitchen utensils, cosmetic products, ready made clothing, processed or luxury foods, and personal effects.

Not only the vendors of ready made goods are reliant on urban sources for their inputs. Small manufacturers in rural centers draw a high proportion of their input materials, tools, and equipment from urban suppliers as well. This is especially true for petty manufacturers of metal goods. Apart from a few artisans who have retained the knowledge of metallurgy, all rural blacksmiths and metal implement makers use iron or steel obtained from urban sources, much of it being "recycled" metal from discarded oil drums, automobile bodies, and roofing material. Even the makers of tools obtain high quality tempered steel from discarded automobile leaf springs. Makers of rubber sandals often use worn auto tires, while manufacturers of bed frames use inner tubes. This aspect of intermediate manufacturing technology has been well documented in previous studies.[5]

Effects of Extended Family Ties and Circular Migration on Purchases from Nonfarm Enterprises

Since colonial times, labor migration from rural areas of Kenya has featured a circular pattern, with migrants remaining for short periods in the city and returning periodically for visits to their extended families in their rural home areas. Although the pattern was enforced during the colonial period by the *kipande* system, it still continues among voluntary migrants from many areas.[6] The effect of circular migration on purchases from rural nonfarm enterprises is not accurately known, but information collected during the nonfarm survey conveys the impression that it is not inconsequential. The sojourning migrants will often buy needed supplies to take back to the city whilst on periodic visits to their rural home areas, thereby taking advantage of lower rural prices. Judging by the produce loaded on vehicles seen returning to Nairobi, such purchases made on periodic rural visits constitute an important source of demand, at least in Central and Eastern provinces.

This relationship between rural production and urban demand can be expressed as an employment multiplier. Louis Meunch has attempted to quantify the direct and indirect multipliers existing

---

5. Kenneth King, *The African Artisan* (London: Heinemann, 1977).

6. W. Elkan, op. cit.

between formal and informal urban labor.[7] The direct multiplier is associated with subcontracting and input purchasing that is carried on between the formal and informal sectors, while consumer expenditures on the products of these sectors constitute important indirect multipliers. Meunch concludes that the informal sector magnifies the employment of the urban formal sector by 45 percent, while informal employment itself accounts for one-third of the total employment in Kenyan cities.[8] It is reasonable to deduce that somewhat similar multipliers operate between the rural nonfarm sector and the urban sector.

Apart from technical skills and the cash brought back with them to rural areas, urban workers, including those who do not follow the pattern of circular migration or frequent rural visits, commonly remit part of their earnings to relatives in rural areas. Remittances from relatives account for over 8 percent of household income at the national level.[9] Data obtained in the Central Province Survey confirm that such remittances are substantial, even from among those engaged in rural nonfarm activities. As shown, the average remittance for rural nonfarm entrepreneurs was KShs 165 per month. The effect of these remittances is to augment the cash brought back by returning urban laborers on their periodic visits to their rural families. The injection of more cash into the rural economy consequently increases trading activity in the small market centers that supply rural households.

The negative side of the rural-urban migration "equation" is discussed by Collier and Rempel.[10] They point to the costs borne by the rural community as a result of such migration, including the rural income foregone by the migrants, the costs of urban subsistence and job search, and the social costs associated with uprooting from their familiar community. However, they also mention that technological diffusion into the rural nonfarm sector occurs as a result of return by workers temporarily employed in the urban informal sector.

---

7. Louis Meunch, "A Final Demand Approach to the Informal Sector and Implications for Public Policies," in *The Informal Sector in Kenya,* ed. S.B. Westley and D. Kabagambe, Institute for Development Studies Occasional Paper no. 25 (Nairobi: University of Nairobi, 1977), pp. 5-34.

8. Ibid., p. 26.

9. Republic of Kenya, Central Bureau of Statistics, *Integrated Rural Survey 1974-75: Basic Report* (Nairobi: Government Printer, 1977) table 8.8, p. 56.

10. Valerie G. Collier and Henry Rempel, "The Divergence of Private from Social Costs in Rural Urban Migration: A Case Study of Nairobi," in *Papers on the Kenyan Economy: Performance, Problems and Policies* (Nairobi: Heinemann, 1981), pp. 228-237.

Investments in Nonfarm Enterprises by Urban Businessmen

Private investments by urban businessmen and civil servants acting on their own behalf are again not capable of being precisely gauged but appear substantial from available indicators. The data for Central Province presented earlier showed clearly that initial capital for investment in nonfarm enterprises came mostly from savings by entrepreneurs and their relatives, a proportion of whom have urban businesses. This is part of the pattern of indigenous capitalization in Kenya remarked on by other writers. In addition, civil servants in the upper echelons of government and the parastatals invest substantial amounts in private enterprises in both urban and rural areas. They are permitted to do this legally as a result of the recommendation to Cabinet by the Ndegwa Commission[11] which saw positive benefits to the country from allowing public servants to engage in business activities.

Competition between Nonfarm Enterprises and Urban Businesses

The undercutting of rural small enterprises by large urban and transnational businesses is a central theme of Dependency Theory. This is one of the mechanisms whereby core regions dominate the periphery of Third World countries. As far as the nonfarm sector is concerned, it is apparent that not all activities feel this pressure from urban competitors to the same extent, and some are quite able to hold their own against it. Bienefield argues that there are three circumstances in which the informal sector (in this instance the rural nonfarm sector) survives: (1) where technologies are not available to permit mechanization and mass production; (2) where markets are too small and fragmented for the formal sector to operate profitably; (3) where the formal sector subcontracts to, or makes purchases from, the rural nonfarm sector (this would include Government purchases).[12]

Relations with the Urban Informal Sector

The urban informal sector in Kenya, as we have noted previously, has been the subject of much analysis since the ILO Report of 1972. The work of William House has in particular been useful in providing a detailed description of the sector and of its

---

11. Colin Leys, op. cit., p. 193.

12. See Bienefield, op. cit. In Kenya, the activities which have been able to withstand outside competition include rural transportation (matatu taxis have all but put out of business some of the large country bus lines), forms of agroprocessing not sensitive to "prestige" image-making by urban manufacturers, traditional products like snuff and herbal remedies, certain services, and small household utensils suited to rural living (jikos, pangas, and jembes). With the aid of protective legislation engineered by vigorous lobbying, transnational corporations have been successful in ousting or undercutting local rural producers of ready made clothing, shoes, and some household items.

relations with the urban formal sector and with the economy in
general.[13] Little is said by any researchers, however, concerning
the relationsips (if any) between the nonfarm sector and the urban
informal sector. We attempt such an assessment here but caution the
reader that much of the information is indirect and inferential in
nature. The main relationships recognized are: (1) the rural
nonfarm sector supplies inputs to the urban informal sector, (2) it
also supplies trained and untrained labor for the urban informal
sector, (3) the urban informal sector supplies inputs of materials
and technology to the rural nonfarm sector, and (4) the two sectors
are to some extent competitive for the same markets. Some of these
linkages and relationships perhaps help to explain why these two
sectors were confused and their distinctions blurred in previous
writings. Both share similar entrepreneurial, employment, and
operational characteristics and compete in some ways for the same
markets. But there the similarities do (and should) end.

In Nairobi, where most studies of the informal sector have
been done, the sector is very large, but concentrated in specific
areas--some central, some peripheral. Market areas on the urban
fringe such as Dagoretti Corners attract some rural residents, while
in more central locations such as Pumwani, the proportion of urban
wage employees among the customers is undoubtedly higher (although
the concentration of informal sector stalls--especially clothing
stalls--near the country bus terminal is noteworthy).

Urban informal scrap metal dealers supply a part of the needs
of rural nonfarm implement and tool manufacturers. Sheet metal,
leaf springs, wire, nails and screws, and other metal parts make
their way into nonfarm rural products in this fashion. New products
and appropriate technologies for informal manufacturing also tend to
originate in the urban informal sector and then diffuse into rural
areas. Examples include bicycle pillion seats and maizecutters
which were first produced in Nairobi's informal manufacturing
area.[14]

Certain raw material requirements of the urban informal sector
are purchased from the rural nonfarm sector; examples include ready
tanned animal hides and leather, wooden handles for tools, charcoal,
cord and twine, and woven baskets for shipping goods. In addition,
many young rural residents, fresh from apprenticeship training with
a rural craftsman, arrive in Nairobi hoping to find lucrative
employment in the urban informal sector. In this way, the urban

13. William House, (1981), op. cit.

14. Kenneth King, op. cit.

informal sector has access to a pool of partly skilled or unskilled labor and a small number of skilled and innovative craftsmen or entrepreneurs. On the other hand, a small amount of subcontracting takes place among petty manufacturers with both urban and rural businesses being the beneficiaries in different cases.

In other important ways, the urban informal sector is competitive with the rural nonfarm sector rather than linked functionally with it. In the city, the informal sector has the advantages of being agglomerated near a large market and of being near to sources of processed materials, centers of capital accumulation, and a large pool of available labor. The urban informal sector thus has superior access for some inputs such as scrap metal and can undercut prices of the rural nonfarm sector in certain product lines, helping in this way to further the effects of urban dominance and economic centralization. But the urban informal sector suffers as well from its location: urban administrators, fearing the effects of unbridled competition by the informal sector on the favored formal sector, embarrased by its disorderly appearance and its questionable modus operandi, and perhaps mistakenly believing that it is nothing but a troublesome dormitory for the urban employed, have periodically attempted to raze the areas where it operates. Alternately, they have from time to time tried to push them to the outskirts of the city, where they will be out of sight and out of mind. The very nature of the urban informal sector dictates that some activities must reappear in the very visible and/or central spaces and thoroughfares frequented by the urban formal sector workers who are its main market, for without their custom the urban informal sector could not long exist.

Attempts at suppression of the urban informal sector in the past have been notably unsucessful. The bulldozers have no sooner done their destructive work on the temporary dwellings and workshops than these lean-to shacks are rebuilt, perhaps at another urban location in the first instance, but eventually on the same undeveloped urban sites as previously occupied. More than a decade ago the ILO denounced the folly of such harassment and pointed to the development potential of the urban informal sector. However it would be a mistake to give preferential treatment to the urban informal sector in circumstances where *the rural nonfarm sector remains a viable alternative*. Favoring metropolitan development will result in the same problems of overcrowding and deterioration of living conditions that are evident today in metropolises elsewhere in the Third World, especially in Latin America.

The competitive positions of the rural and urban informal sectors for satisfying urban demand are compared by Meunch,[15] who comes down on the side of the urban informal sector. He acknowledges that rural areas have advantages of cheap factor costs of land, buildings, and labor, but claims that these are offset by higher costs of imported material inputs and higher costs of transportation to urban markets for finished goods such as furniture. Meunch notes that middlemen are involved in distribution of rural goods to urban consumers which, in his view, detracts from the efficiency of the sector. He makes no mention, however, of the serious deficiencies of the urban informal sector in areas of industrial over-concentration, or of the criticism by Leys concerning its contribution to exploitation of labor by transnational capital. Also, Meunch mistakenly believes that the urban informal sector is larger than the rural nonfarm sector.[16]

Relationships with the Public Sector

Until the last few years, the overriding attitude of the public sector in Kenya toward the rural nonfarm sector could best be characterized as one of non-recognition and consequently of benign neglect. Certain decisions taken by the government and the parastatals did, of course, have gratuitous effects on the rural nonfarm sector. But since the mid-1970s, the Government has moved to redress its oversight, beginning with surveys to expand its understanding of the sector, followed by official pronouncements about stimulation of the sector, written into the 1979-1983 *Development Plan*. It is clear that the Government, and through it the whole public and parastatal sector, can have a potentially great impact for good or ill on the rural nonfarm sector. We review some actual and potential impacts below.

One of the main ways in which the government has produced direct effects on the rural nonfarm sector is via legislation that has been either beneficial or detrimental to interests in rural areas. Three examples are: protection for large-scale industry, wage control, and technical education. Thus, legislation to prohibit the importation of second-hand clothing has had a negative impact on mobile clothing vendors who dealt in such goods and on the rural tailors who altered clothing on a custom-order basis. This restriction was imposed at the instigation of large, transnational textile manufacturers in urban areas, who feared the competition of

15. Louis Meunch, op. cit.
16. Ibid., p. 13.

the petty clothing vendors. Legislation on wages has resulted in a somewhat higher minimum wage in urban areas than for rural areas. By a mechanism described in the Harris-Todaro model,[17] this has ensured that there is a continuous stream of rural emigrants seeking the higher paying (but notoriously elusive) urban jobs, thereby exacerbating problems of urban overcrowding and underemployment. Until recent years education has stressed academic subjects rather than teaching agriculture and craft-related skills which, at least in rural areas, are far more suited to the milieu in which most school leavers will work. This, as we have seen, obliges most nonfarm artisans to learn their trade "on the job" in rural areas.[18]

Ways in which the Government may potentially affect the future of the rural nonfarm sector are numerous. Some of these potential interventions in the areas of financial aid, training, technical education, extension service, protection, and demand stimulation are outlined below. It is a sufficiently important topic that we make it the subject of the next chapter in which we outline in fairly specific terms the prescriptive approaches that the Kenyan Government might take in order to develop the rural nonfarm sector and rural areas in general.

---

17. See M.P. Todaro, "A Model of Labor Migration and Urban Unemployment in Less Developed Countries," *American Economic Review* 69 (1969): 138-148.

18. Recently the Government has focused more attention on stimulation of the Rural Craft Training Centers, the successors of the Village Polytechnics located in medium-sized settlements. See: David Barker and Alan Ferguson, "The Craft Training Center as a Rural Mobilization Policy in Kenya," *Rural Africana* 12-13 (Winter-Spring 1981-82): 75-90.

CHAPTER VII

FROM DESCRIPTION TO PRESCRIPTION:
TOWARD A NEW RURAL ORDER

Our analysis in this study reinforces the mounting criticism of past theoretical and policy emphases which have favored urban-industrial development in most underdeveloped countries. With the wisdom of hindsight, these policies have been shown to be largely misplaced. ok. wont be long. is not easy to duplicate the formula for growth propelled by urban industries which was so successful in the nineteenth century in presently rich, Western countries. Recent attempts to restructure the modes of production or control of Third World economies which do not, at the same time, redress this urban bias will face serious difficulties. An alternative formula, which puts priority on rural development is, we believe, a more promising recipe for economic advancement in the majority of underdeveloped countries. But it follows that, since the present system of rural production is creaking under the strain of population growth, extensive rural transformation will be necessary if substantial economic development is to be achieved.

Hitherto, most proposals for rural transformation and development have focused almost exclusively on agriculture. This is understandable, given the dominance of this sector in employment and wealth creation. However, Anderson and Lieserson, among others, have provided extensive evidence testifying to the importance of the rural nonfarm sector which, like agriculture, must be equally involved in this transformation if development goals are to be achieved.[1] Clearly, given the interdependencies discussed in chapter 5, the two sectors cannot act independently: changes in the organization of the rural nonfarm sector must necessarily mirror changes in agricultural production. We will, therefore, briefly outline the changes in agricultural production which, we suggest, will bring about the desired pattern of development. In so doing, we do not explore the political feasibility of these proposals,

---

1. D. Anderson and M.W. Leiserson, "Rural Nonfarm Employment in Developing Countries," *Economic Development and Cultural Change* 28 (1980): 227-248.

beyond recognising the force of Colin Leys' comment in his critique
of the ILO Report:[2] Leys pointed to the improbability of Kenya's
national bourgeoisie taking the initiative to introduce the sweeping
reforms recommended by the ILO, which may, if implemented,
impoverish themselves. Yet, we would argue, reform is the result of
a process in which all concerned groups, and not just the ruling
elite, review and negotiate on issues of national development. The
essence of agricultural reform in a country such as Kenya, which has
a shortage of good farmland as well as increasing rural population
densities in the few high potential areas, must be to maximize gross
agricultural product and, at the same time, to distribute those
benefits as widely as possible amongst the rural population. That
requires first of all an intensification of production methods and,
in some cases, local agricultural specialization on crops which have
the greatest comparative advantage.

Intensification of production methods to increase output and
meet our equity criterion requires the continued widespread use of
labor-intensive methods using relatively simple technologies.
Though it is evident that profitability per hectare is generally
higher on large farms using modern capital intensive technologies,
gross yields are higher on small farms using simpler technologies.[3]
Moreover the market prices of imported agricultural implements and
fertilizers are below their shadow prices which suggests that there
are at present hidden subsidies which benefit mechanization.
Removal of implicit subsidies such as low import duties on such
machinery should result in a resource re-allocation in favor of more
labor-intensive methods. Though this may be politically unpopular
in some quarters (especially large-scale farmers), the application
of labor-intensive methods will require the sub-division of large
holdings in high potential areas.

The issue then arises whether smallholder production should be
focussed exclusively on food crop production. With some
reservations, we acknowledge that there are very substantial
economic advantages to be gained from agricultural specialization in
cash crops, which are jointly accounted for by the principle of
comparative advantage and the creation of various agglomeration
economies. Against this, however, are the risks to the peasant of
serious food shortages attendant upon a wholesale change to
commercial crops for export. Not surprisingly, in the face of such

2. Colin Leys, op. cit.

3. Peter Wyeth, "Economic Development in Kenyan Agriculture," in Tony
Killick, ed., op. cit., pp. 299-310.

uncertainties, the farmers have been reluctant to concentrate fully on cash crops. To encourage more farmers to specialize--where such specialization is ecologically sound--the Government needs to minimize the risks of food shortages by carrying substantial reserves of essential food staples including maize and rice and by restoring confidence shaken by recent food crises. In the short term, increased semi-subsistence food output in some regions is a necessary interim step before such a climate of confidence can be achieved.

There are good grounds for arguing that the changes in agricultural production outlined above will have a highly stimulative effect on the rural nonfarm sector. Increased agricultural output will require larger inputs to agriculture from the rural nonfarm sector; it will also stimulate agroprocessing and, by increasing disposable incomes, will have a substantial indirect multiplier effect on the nonfarm sector. Whereas the import content of inputs to large scale farming is high, small scale farming relies more on local inputs, as was shown in this study. Local interdependencies will therefore be fostered by an expansion of small-farm cash cropping. Also, in contrast with the consumption pattern of wealthy landowners, which favor imported items, land redistribution will encourage the consumption of locally produced goods.

At the heart of this discussion is the contention that rural transformation will be most successful if it is *demand* led. The following specific proposals reflect this emphasis on the demand side, but we also make reference to certain supply side considerations which must be incorporated into the paradigm for development.

Demand-Side Policies to Aid the Rural Nonfarm Sector

To expand the concepts in the model summarized above, we outline some specific policy measures that would either directly or indirectly promote the expansion of the rural nonfarm sector. We consider these policies to be entirely feasible, even though some may not be readily acceptable to particular interest groups. All of them may be implemented in Third World countries without a complete restructuring of existing modes of production. Nevertheless we accept Killick's argument that effective planning requires a realistic view of politics and decision making.[4] Thus the

---

4. Tony Killick, "The Possibilities of Development Planning," *Oxford Economic Papers* 28 (1976): 161-183; H. Myint, "The Demand Approach to Economic Development," *Review of Economic Studies* 27 (1960): 124-132.

implementation of the proposed policies would require considerable
influence being brought to bear upon sensitive points in the
machinery of government.

In the realm of land reform, the following measures are needed
to relieve rural stagnation and reduce rural to urban migration:
(1) prohibiting further land accumulation and farm purchases beyond
the acreage required for a family farm, where that acreage will vary
according to land potential, unless such farms are to be
incorporated, owned, and managed as a cooperative farm under the
auspices of the Ministry of Cooperative Development; (2) reducing
existing disparities in the size of land holdings, especially those
that are owned by absentee landlords; this will permit the
redistribution of land toward more labor-intensive farm units; (3)
ecologically sensitive areas, such as forested watersheds and
semi-arid rangelands, need to be treated separately from the
high-density peasant farming areas, with livestock, tourism, and
other extensive land uses integrated in multi-use management
schemes. Land clearing by agriculturalists in such sensitive areas
should be discouraged vigorously.

A review of controls on internal transportation and pricing of
foodstuffs is recommended to promote freer interregional movement of
food for rural consumption. These changes should help Kenya to
avoid local famines in food deficit regions by encouraging efficient
distribution of food surpluses produced in other regions of the
country. Excessive interregional price variations would be
prevented by a flexible price stabilization program, involving
guaranteed floor and ceiling prices maintained through government
purchases, storage, and sale of stocks of affected commodities.[5] The
stimulus so provided to small farmers should create expansion in the
rural nonfarm sector which, as we have stressed in this study, owes
its main existence to supplying the small farm sector.

Policies Limiting Competition by Urban Sectors for the Markets of the Rural Nonfarm Sector

Agglomeration economies, superior access to information
channels and to markets, and urban biases in government expenditures
give advantages to urban formal and informal producers that are not
available to rural nonfarm enterprises. However, certain
diseconomies of urban production are not borne by urban producers
themselves, but are spread over the national economy as a whole;
these are in effect a form of subsidy to urban producers not enjoyed
by small rural producers. An example would be the greater cost of

5. See J. Heyer, D. Ireri, and J. Moris, op. cit., 1970,

urban public services due to higher urban wage levels (and paid out of taxes collected largely in rural areas). Food price stabilization schemes have also generally benefitted urban dwellers by keeping down wage-led cost inflation. This, too, is a subsidy which lowers the operating costs of urban firms. Raising the price of food products closer to free market levels will do much to resolve this problem: it would eliminate the subsidy and shift the terms of trade in favor of rural areas. The effects of such measures will be to make rural living and rural production more attractive, reducing the competitive edge of urban producers and discouraging rural residents from migrating to the metropolis with its higher costs of living. The rural nonfarm sector can be expected to benefit from such developments.

Another area of central concern is commodity production by transnational corporations. Studies by Langdon and Kaplinsky indicate that these firms use such devices as management fees, over-invoicing, and internal artificial prices to repatriate the majority of their profits.[6] This restricts local capital accumulation. Local firms, in contrast, tend to reinvest their profits locally. This is not, however, intended as unqualified support for import substitution since such a policy frequently results in high costs to rural consumers as a consequence of over-protected, inefficient urban branch plants. Inefficient urban industries that cannot survive without government subsidies and/or monopolistic devices such as protective legislation, import restrictions, and licensing restrictions generally result in high costs to the consumer. In some instances the infant industry argument has some justification, but very commonly this form of protectionism fosters inefficiency.

Forced industrial decentralization to designated growth poles and rural areas when economic location factors dictate otherwise is not recommended. It promotes economic inefficency. Moreover, the owners of decentralized plants often demand in return the monopoly status and protective legislation mentioned above. Yet, such firms usually conduct only a minimal search amongst alternative locations, and rarely even consider sites outside of Nairobi.[7] There is, therefore, a good case for drawing attention to decentralized

---

6. Steven Langdon, "Multi-National Corporations, Taste Transfer and Underdevelopment: A Case Study from Kenya," *Review of African Political Economy* 21 (1975): 12-35; Steven Langdon, *Multinational Corporations in the Political Economy of Kenya* (New York: St. Martin's Press, 1981); Raphael Kaplinsky, ed., *Readings on the Multinational Corporation in Kenya* (Nairobi: Oxford University Press, 1978).

7. Clay Wescott and Glen Norcliffe, "Towards a Locational Policy for Manufacturing Industry in Kenya," in Glen Norcliffe and Tom Pinfold, eds. op. cit., 1981, pp. 79-109.

locations in the application process.

The government can improve the competitive position of rural nonfarm enterprises by reorienting its programs to give greater emphasis to projects in farming areas and small market centers. For instance, Nairobi has for long received a disproportionate amount of public expenditure, both in capital and recurrent spending. There is, therefore, a strong argument in terms of equity for a substantial shift of public investment in favor of rural areas. A larger allocation should therefore be given to such projects as rural water supply, rural access roads, all-weather roads linking regional markets into "market circuits," technical training facilities (stressing crafts, agroprocessing, crop cultivation, and livestock care), watershed management programs, and programs to transfer appropriate technology to agriculture, rural manufacturing, and rural business. Rural credit, farm input supply schemes, market support facilities, and community development programs are other areas in which Government efforts need to be reorganized to give greater prominence to rural areas.

"Supply-Side" Policies to Expand the Rural Nonfarm Sector

The main objective of policies on the supply side is to expand the capacity for employment and productivity in the nonfarm sector. The most promising activities on which to focus such strategies are those involving small-scale manufacturing, since such activities have a stronger need for training, credit, technological support, and infrastructure than is the case for wholesale and retail trading and for services.

Existing Government policies and programs to assist small-scale rural industrialization are dealt with in detail elsewhere.[8] Here, we put forward some ideas which lead in the direction of expanded rural nonfarm activity, and especially of rural industry. Policies and programs will be considered under four headings: training programs, loan schemes, infrastructure, and rural extension programs.

Training Programs

As our study has shown, most employees and operators of rural enterprises are trained on the job as apprentices. A small, but apparently growing number are being trained at Craft Training Centers.[9] We suggest, however, that formal training programs with such things as certificate requirements are not the best way of

8. G. Norcliffe, D. Freeman, and N. Miles, 1980, op. cit., pp. 42-86.

9. David Barker and Alan Ferguson, op. cit.

preparing rural entrepreneurs and artisans. The best form of
training, we feel, is on-the-job. We therefore suggest that small
enterprises should be encouraged to engage new apprentices by means
of a Government labor subsidy. The subsidy would have to be small
to avoid abuse, but a modest payment to a recognized master
craftsman in return for taking on an apprentice for a specified
training period should generate many new apprentice positions.
Enterprises located in Nairobi or Mombasa could be excluded from
this scheme. Its feasibility could be tested through pilot programs
in a selected district.

Turning to the Craft Training Centers, the original intention
was that such training facilities and programs be related to local
industrial employment opportunities. By 1979, there were 220 such
centers (then known as Village Polytechnics).[10] There is evidence
that, in some areas, the willingness or capacity of the local
economy to absorb skilled CTC graduates is in question.[11] Such
facilities should probably not be kept open if there is a lack of
local interest. The really important links for craft trainees are
not with the central government, but with local industry. The
existing practice of using contract work to provide funds and
practical experience should be expanded into a form of in-course
workshop in which students alternate between classroom and industry.
Many CTCs already include visits to rural workshops; it would
therefore seem possible to expand them further through small
training fees paid to village entrepreneurs who agree to engage CTC
trainees for, say, a month. Again, a pilot scheme could be used to
test this program. Also, the newly tried concept of cooperative
work-groups of CTC graduates in rural areas has promise.

Loan Schemes

The main problems with existing Government loan schemes are
that they do not effectively reach down to very small manufacturers;
many of the loans from institutions such as the Industrial and
Commercial Development Corporation are for construction businesses
and traders, and not for small scale rural industry; there is,
moreover, a high default rate amongst loan recipients, so that many
of the "revolving" loan funds could more realistically be described
as sinking funds. Efforts to collect payments from loan-defaulters
often appear to be less than determined.

---

10. Ibid., p. 77.
11. Ibid., p. 81.

In view of the above problems and because urban banks have been notably reluctant in the past to make loans to small farmers, it would seem necessary and desirable to change existing policies so as to extend access to credit facilities to peasants and rural entrepreneurs. This could be done both through the expansion of commercial banking facilities and by modifying the current government and parastatal procedures for extending credit. Though the government has to play an important role in this process, the objective should be primarily to expand the role of the commercial and cooperative sectors. The expansion of banking and loan facilities in small towns (serving surrounding rural areas) should have the twofold effect of providing a channel for local savings (ensuring that they are retained in rural investments) and a source of commercial credit. Since these rural branches might not at first be profitable, it may be necessary for the government to insist on such expansions, with profitable metropolitan branches subsidizing rural branches. The raising of interest rates on bank deposits would also have a stimulative effect on the rate of saving in rural areas.

In the short run, before the commercial and cooperative banking network is enlarged, small loan schemes should operate on a more selective basis. There is clearly an abundance of many types of business in most small towns, particularly in the commercial sector. Williams and McClintock state:

> There is an excess of many types of business particularly on the general retail side, and a lack of more specialized businesses. Yet often general retail businesses are receiving loans, which results in wasteful use of public money, and is probably to the disadvantage of rural people.[12]

The best criterion for loan selection, in our view, is the local multiplier effect of a loan. Loans for imported tools or imported wholesale goods are not likely to have much local impact: loans for construction using local materials might have greater local multiplier effects. Unfortunately virtually no research has been done on such local multipliers and their impact on rural nonfarm activities: we feel that such research should be given higher priority.

Loans to small scale enterprises should be concentrated in the hands of District Joint Loan Boards (DJLBs), who, in the past, have been notably successful in distributing credit to rural enterprises. The Industrial and Commercial Development Corporation (ICDC), however, was originally established to develop formal industry

---

12. K.G. Williams and H. McClintock, "District Development Planning and Growth Centre Stategies: Employment Implications for Kenyan Planning" (unpublished report to the United Kingdom Social Science Research Council, 1979), p. ii.

through equity participation and loans. Responsibility for small
scale enterprise was added at a later date. It would seem desirable
that ICDC concentrate its energies on loan schemes for formal sector
industry and commerce, leaving the loans for very small producers to
be handled by DJLBs that are suitably expanded and strengthened.
There are two advantages to this. First, DJLBs exclusively handle
small loans and therefore have developed a perception of the role of
these loans that is different from that of the ICDC (with its broad
range of responsibilities). Second, the criteria that DJLBs apply
can vary from district to district (ICDC tends to use more
standardized criteria). Thus we are, in essence, advocating a
decentralization of responsibility for small scale loans until
cooperative and commercial banks are able to assume more of this
role.

Infrastructure

Present efforts to expand the network of rural feeder roads
and rural water and electricity supply lines seem entirely
appropriate. We support such efforts and approve of the recent
trend to decentralize decision-making on infrastructure development
to the District level. The aspect of infrastructure that we feel
needs changing is the role of Rural Industrial Development Centers
(RIDCs), which are large modern facilities administered by a
parastatal agency of the Government. The main role of RIDCs could
be changed to convert them into cooperative workshops. We suggest
that this workshop role of the RIDCs be enhanced, that their
credit-giving role be shared with District Joint Loan Boards, and
that the main responsibility for education and extension services
for rural industry be transferred to the rural Craft Training
Centers discussed above.

RIDCs have been built on too large and formal a scale to serve
small scale rural industry very effectively. They are like small
industrial estates, and this formal orientation should be accepted
and built upon. Making them into cooperative workshops is merely
recognizing what is currently their most useful role. Tools should
be shared on a "user-pay" basis. In expanding this workshop role,
we make two further suggestions: (1) that RIDCs enlarge their
supplier role to become a main source of inputs and equipment to
rural industry (thus RIDCs would carry stocks of wood, scrap and
other metal, cloth, hardware, and basic tools needed by artisans)
and (2) that RIDCs assume a marketing role, particularly with a view
to helping rural producers sell more of their products in larger

towns and in Nairobi. The possibility of promoting certain items (particularly craft products) in export markets should also be examined.

Extension Programs

The major responsibility for craft and trade extension programs should be transferred--along with classroom and workshop craft training--to CTCs. In our view, education and extension for rural industry have much in common and should be brought together. Both should be handled on an informal basis, and as we stress in this study, a major emphasis should be placed on workshop experience in local workshops. Since there are ten times as many CTCs as RIDCs, and new craft training centers are being completed at an average rate of around 30 per year, the potential exists for much wider impacts if information about new products and tools is diffused through CTCs. This diffusion process wil be even more effective if new CTCs are connected with the various institutions and organizations working with appropriate technologies so as consciously to maximize the dissemination of useful information.

Conclusion: Facing the Future

The rural nonfarm sector will be an important part of Kenya's future, no matter how problem-ridden that future may be. The thousands of Kenyans who are already involved in this sector have developed it into an indispensable part of the rural economy, interdependent with peasant agriculture. For the very poor, it is a way of raising cash income to provide for some of their needs and wants that could not otherwise be met. For the landless, it is often their whole livelihood. For the full-time farmer, it is a source of cheap goods and services that may, perhaps, mean the difference between continued successful farming and selling out to a rich neighbor. For the better educated and more fortunate--those with capital and influence--it may be a source of large profits and the means of a comfortable life-style.

Overall, the nonfarm sector strengthens the fabric of rural society and promotes its economic cohesion. It offers an alternative to urban migration for those without the prospect of land inheritance. We therefore view the nonfarm sector as a positive element of rural Kenya. While this sector remains vigorous and strong, it checks urban hegemony. It provides rural residents with a degree of choice and flexibility that they would otherwise be denied. In short, the rural nonfarm sector is not--of this we are convinced--simply a poor country cousin of the urban informal sector so often condemned as an agent of economic exploitation and deprivation.

Realism dictates that the nonfarm sector's limitations must also be recognized. Most notably, it cannot be a leader in rural development--that must be the role of agriculture and resource industries. A major part of it is dependent on outside sources of processed inputs and technology, so complete regional closure and full self-sufficiency are unattainable and would, in any case, be out of place in modern Kenya.

Interregional variations in nature and structure of the rural nonfarm sector make it difficult to plan on a broad scale. Indeed, to some analysts, the concept of planning for so patently fragmented and informal a sector is a contradiction in itself. However, we feel there is much that a committed government can do to enhance and improve the functioning of this sector as a development instrument. This is particularly true if planning is interpreted, in Friedmann's terms, as "social learning," or territorially-organized, rural grass-roots planning--the epitome of "planning from the ground up."[13]

Critical parts of this strategy of planning from below are the development and application of spatial concepts and strategies, intertwined with regionally and ecologically sound programs for improving productivity and meeting basic needs. In the absence of such programs aimed at promoting rural development, the current steady flow of rural-to-urban migration and the parallel centralization of capital and power may in future swell to a flood. In short, while not intending to portray the rural nonfarm sector as a cure-all for the ills of Third World underdevelopment, we confidently assert that it has a valuable role to play.

---

13. John Friedmann, "Regional Planning for Rural Mobilization in Africa," *Rural Africana* 12-13 (Winter-Spring 1981-82): 3-20.

APPENDIX

The Rural Nonfarm Surveys
The Preliminary Household Survey, 1977: A Nonfarm Activity Count

The sample for the survey was drawn from the frame designed
for the national Integrated Rural Survey, covering selected sample
areas in all provinces except North-Eastern Province and Nairobi.
About twenty households from each of 118 sample areas were surveyed
during the period December 1976-January 1977. A total of 2232
households were interviewed. Although the household is the basic
unit of this survey, it is not the only organizational unit for
non-farm activities. Enterprise units, for example, are an
alternative form of organization. Therefore, the sample cannot be
construed as covering all organizational types of non-farm activity.
It undoubtedly covers an extremely large part of the rural non-farm
sector in Kenya, however, where the majority of income-earning units
are in fact small scale farmsteads on which certain supplementary
activities are carried out.

The focus of the survey was a target population comprising all
persons in the sample households over the age of 15 who were not
attending school full time. Responses were sought to the questions:
1. Have any activities other than crop production and livestock
   rearing been carried on in this household for more than a
   month in the past year?
2. If "yes," name the activity or activities.

The enumerator was provided with a questionnaire sheet on which a
detailed list of specific non-farm activities was set out.
Activities mentioned by the respondent were recorded on the
questionnaire sheet as being undertaken by the interviewee's
household. Although the broad categories of the list are based on
the International Standard Industrial Classification, the detailed
breakdown of activities was designed to be particularly relevant to
the rural Kenyan milieu. The survey focused on the kinds of
activities which are more rural and "traditional" in nature, and

160

thus activities which are clearly part of the "formal" sector, such
as teaching, employment in Government, and accountancy, were not
specifically identified on the list.

The list of activities which formed the basis of the
questionnaire is reproduced in table 3.7.

The Supplementary Household Survey, 1977-78: Nonfarm Module No. 2

This survey module was inserted into the ongoing program of
the Integrated Rural Survey being conducted by the Central Bureau of
Statistics. It was designed to obtain information concerning: (1)
rural household purchases of basic needs--specifically those
obtainable from the rural nonfarm sector, such as food, clothing,
shoes, pots and pans, and furniture (beds/tables); and (2) some
characteristics of the operators of nonfarm activities at the
national level. The same sampling frame used for the first IRS
household survey was employed in this case, but there were some
differences in the interview procedure. For example, activities
classified as "formal"--such as, public service workers--were not
excluded as in the case of the first survey. Some categories were
redefined as a result of lessons learned from the earlier module.
Results of the first part of this module--that dealing with
household purchases of nonfarm products--are shown in tables 3.1 to
3.5. Characteristics of the enterprise operators themselves are
shown in tables 3.8 to 3.14. These characteristics include sex,
age, relation to household head, education, literacy, wage, income,
and category of employment of respondents in sampled households.
The response frequency for this part of the module was 527
respondents. This module permits interprovincial comparisons of
these data but, as in the case of other IRS surveys, is invalid for
District-level comparisons due to the relatively small sample size.

*The Central Province Survey of Nonfarm Enterprises in Rural Market
Centers*

The survey was based on a sample of enterprises drawn from
fifty-two rural or small market centers in Central Province. The
first step in selecting the sample was to compile a list of all
those centers classified as rural centers or market centers by the
Physical Planning Department of the Ministry of Lands and
Settlement. The location of these centers was then plotted on a
base map of the province, and a grid system was used to draw a
sample of centers, weighted in accordance with spatial variations in
settlement density. The largest number of sample centers are in
Kiambu District (twenty-five centers), since this is the most

densely settled area of the Province. Eleven centers were selected
in Murang'a District, seven in Nyeri District, while five and four
centers were chosen in Nyandarua and Kirinyaga districts,
respectively.

Within each center, small, roving field teams of interviewers
were instructed to enumerate the enterprises encountered, except in
the cases of general stores (dukas) and open air market enterprises,
where sheer numbers and the repetitive nature of the activities
precluded full enumeration in the larger centers. In such cases, a
systematic sampling procedure was adopted, in which every fourth
enterprise was selected for interview.

Interviews were conducted by four students from the University
of Nairobi who could speak fluently in Kikuyu, Swahili, and English.
The vast majority of the interviews were conducted in Kikuyu. Since
the questionnaire was written in English, the interviewers underwent
a short course in interviewing before going into the field to ensure
that they were translating questions in an identical manner.

To assure maximum accuracy, coding was done in the field by
the two field supervisors immediately after the completion of the
interview. Any obvious errors were corrected at once. Also, the
questionnaire contains a number of crosschecks. Serious
discrepancies were recoded as "don't know." The entire coding and
keypunching was double-checked by the principal researchers, thereby
reducing human and machine errors as far as was possible.

The standard industrial classifications available to us were
not appropriate for the purposes in hand. Such classifications
reflect the workings of the modern sector. It was therefore
necessary to devise a classification tailored to describe the
operating characteristics of what has been called the informal or
the traditional sector. This required a classification that to some
extent reflected local conditions. The major categories of
activity--resource extraction, manufacturing, construction, and so
on--are similar to those found in standard classifications.
However, the activities identified within these categories reflect
the particular nature of this sector. Without modification, the
classification we devised may not be suitable for surveys in other
countries because the informal sector tends to be adapted to local
cultural traditions. A number of repair activities have been
included, since Third World societies typically recycle goods by
repairing them rather than disposing of them.

The main topics addressed in the questionnaire were:
1. The nature of the activities carried on in the enterprise
2. A profile of the operator of the enterprise
3. The operating characteristics of the business
4. Employment structure in the rural nonfarm sector
5. An historical review of the enterprise
6. The present capital structure of the enterprise
7. The technologies used in the production process.

APPENDIX TABLE 1

THE STRUCTURE OF SAMPLE ENTERPRISES

Code No.	Activity	Enterprises		Employment				Depreciated Current Assets			
		Number	%	Total Number[a]	%	average per establishment[b]	Total (KShs.)	%	average per establishment	average per employee
	RESOURCE EXTRACTION (TOTAL)	5	0.6	5	0.3	1.0	47	0.00	9	9
13.		5	0.6	5	0.3	1.0	47	0.00	9	9
	MANUFACTURING (TOTAL)	177	20.8	390.0	25.8	2.2	4,367,503	25.93	24,765	11,199
30.	Posho mills	11	1.2	16.5	1.1	1.5	386,500	2.29	48,312	23,424
31.	Bakeries	1	0.1	2	0.1	2.0	5,000	0.03	5,000	2,500
22.	Butter, cheese and other dairy products	3	0.4	22.5	1.5	7.5	428,000	2.54	142,667	19,022
35.	Pombe brewing	17	2.0	76.5	5.1	4.5	630,950	3.75	64,095	8,248
36.	Other food, beverage and tobacco processing	2	0.2	2	0.1	1.0	1,050	0.01	525	525
37.	Fiber products	1	0.1	1	0.1	1.0	50	0.00	50	50
39.	Weaving, spinning, knitting and dyeing	5	0.6	7.5	0.5	1.5	23,550	0.14	4,710	3,140
40.	Tailoring	57	6.7	81	5.4	1.4	570,585	3.39	10,010	7,044
42.	Animal skin products, incl. shoes	23	2.7	39.5	2.6	1.7	275,436	1.64	11,975	6,973
43.	Sawmills	2	0.2	27	1.8	13.5	530,000	3.15	265,000	19,630
44.	Furniture	32	3.8	77	5.1	2.4	1,232,050	7.31	38,501	16,001

45. Handles, carts and other wood products	2	0.2	3	0.2	1.5	250	0.00	125	83
46. Metal farm implements	2	0.2	2	0.1	1.0	19,500	0.12	9,750	9,750
47. Household utensils (mainly jikos)	14	1.6	23.5	1.6	1.7	107,700	0.64	7,693	4,583
48. Other metal products	3	0.4	7	0.5	2.3	133,000	0.79	44,333	19,000
49. Other manufacturing n.e.s.	2	0.2	2	0.1	1.0	23,883	0.15	11,941	11,941
CONSTRUCTION (TOTAL)	4	0.5	7	0.5	1.8	41,900	0.25	10,475	5,986
50. Cement and stone blocks	1	0.1	1	0.1	1.0	80	0.00	80	80
55. Other building and construction	3	0.4	6	0.4	2.0	41,100	0.24	13,700	6,850
WHOLESALE, RETAIL AND HOTELS (TOTAL)	549	64.5	922.5	61.0	1.7	11,330,543	67.26	20,639	12,282
60. Wholesale	5	0.6	13	0.9	2.6	448,330	2.66	89,666	34,487
61. Clothing vendors	47	5.5	58	3.8	1.2	307,630	1.83	6,545	5,304
62. Dukas	208	24.4	279.5	18.5	1.3	5,655,700	33.57	27,589	20,235
63. Butchers	34	4.0	53.5	3.5	1.6	303,070	1.80	9,776	5,665
64. Petrol stations	9	1.1	28	1.9	3.1	361,497	2.15	40,166	12,911
65. Food Kiosks and meat roasters	28	3.3	42	2.8	1.5	151,800	0.96	5,779	3,852
66. Bars and hotels	110	12.9	298	19.7	2.7	2,975,820	17.67	27,811	9,986
68. Secondhand dealers	1	0.1	1	0.1	1.0	5,000	0.03	5,000	5,000
69. Other retailing	107	12.6	149.5	9.9	1.4	1,111,696	6.60	10,793	7,436

APPENDIX TABLE 1, CONT.

Code No.	Activity	Enterprises		Employment			Depreciated Current Assets			
		Number	%	Total Number	%	average per establishment	Total (KShs.)	%	average per establishment	average per employee
	TRANSPORT, STORAGE AND COMMUNICATIONS (TOTAL)	14	1.6	24.5	1.6	1.8	445,580	2.65	31,827	18,187
71.	Matatu (taxi) operators	10	1.2	20.5	1.4	2.1	439,000	2.61	43,900	21,415
72.	Water carriers	2	0.2	2	0.1	1.0	5,000	0.03	2,500	2,500
74.	Animal-drawn vehicle operators	1	0.1	1	0.1	1.0	1,500	0.01	1,500	1,500
75.	Other transport operators	1	0.1	1	0.1	1.0	80	0.00	80	80
	FINANCIAL AND BUSINESS SERVICES (TOTAL)	1	0.1	1	0.1	1.0	35,000	0.21	35,000	35,000
84.	Other business service	1	0.1	1	0.1	1.0	35,000	0.21	35,000	35,000
	COMMUNITY, SOCIAL AND RELATED SERVICES (TOTAL)	102	12.0	162.5	10.7	1.8	625,048	3.71	6,128	3,846
90.	Midwives and clinics	2	0.2	5	0.3	2.5	8,000	0.04	4,000	1,600
91.	Traditional healers	3	0.4	4	0.3	1.3	3,420	0.02	1,140	855
93.	Clothing and foot-wear reparis	15	1.8	20	1.3	1.3	43,458	0.26	2,897	2,173
94.	Car repairs	8	0.9	37	2.4	4.6	97,150	0.58	12,144	2,626
95.	Bicycle repairs	18	2.1	24.5	1.6	1.4	182,990	1.09	10,166	7,469

96. Tool and machinery repairs	1	0.1	1	0.1	1.0	400	0.00	400	400
97. Other repairs	14	1.5	18	1.2	1.3	74,830	0.44	5,345	4,157
98. Barbers and hair-dressers	19	2.2	23	1.5	1.2	53,950	0.32	3,372	2,346
99. Other services	22	2.6	30.0	2.0	1.4	160,850	0.95	7,311	5,361
GRAND TOTAL	852	100.0	1,512.5	100.0	1.8	16,845,621	100.0	19,772	11,138

[a]Part-time employees were counted as 0.5 employees.

[b]Due to incomplete responses, the number of establishments used to compute these averages may be less than the number shown in the first column.

168

APPENDIX TABLE 2

COMPARISON OF RURAL INDUSTRY IN RURAL HOUSEHOLDS AND
IN MARKET CENTRES: CENTRAL PROVINCE, 1977
(Percent of employment, by activity)

	Rural Household	Market Center
Woodcutters	3.3	2.0
Bamboo and reedcutters	0.8	-
Fishermen	0.8	-
Mining and quarrying	2.5	-
TOTAL, RESOURCE EXTRACTION	7.4	2.0
Posho mills	1.6	4.3
Dairy products	1.6	1.2
Coffee processing	2.5	-
Pombe brewing	9.8	6.7
Tobacco products	0.8	-
Bakeries	-	0.4
Other food industries, n.e.s.	0.8	0.8
TOTAL, FOOD, BEVERAGES AND TOBACCO	17.2	13.4
Sisal bags and mats	2.5	0.4
Reed bags, baskets and mats	3.3	-
Weaving, spinning, knitting and dyeing	0.8	2.0
Clothing	4.9	22.4
Animal skin products (including shoes)	0.8	9.1
TOTAL, PLANT, ANIMAL AND FIBRE PRODUCTS, AND CLOTHING	12.3	33.9
Cement and stone blocks	1.6	0.4
Other construction, n.e.s.	0.8	1.2
TOTAL, CONSTRUCTION	2.5	1.6

APPENDIX TABLE 2, CONT.

	Rural Household	Market Center
Sawmills	4.9	0.8
Charcoal making	19.7	–
Building poles	0.8	–
Furniture	5.7	12.6
Wooden handles	1.6	0.8
Gourds and containers	1.6	–
TOTAL, WOOD PRODUCTS	34.4	14.2
Metal farm implements	–	0.8
Household utensils (including jikos)	3.3	5.5
Blacksmiths	1.6	–
Other metal products	–	1.2
TOTAL, METAL PRODUCTS	4.9	7.5
Car and truck repairs	1.6	3.1
Tool and machinery repairs	0.8	0.4
Furniture repairs	2.5	–
Clothing and footwear repairs	4.1	5.9
Bicycle repairs	–	7.1
Other repairs	–	5.5
TOTAL, REPAIRING	9.0	22.0
Matatu operators	5.7	3.9
Water carriers	1.6	0.8
Truck and lorry operators	3.3	–
Animal-drawn vehicle operators	–	0.4
Other transport operators	1.6	0.4
TOTAL, TRANSPORT	12.3	5.5
GRAND TOTAL	100.0	100.0

SOURCES: Freeman and Norcliffe, 1979, Table 6; Norcliffe and Freeman, 1979, Table 1.

BIBLIOGRAPHY

Amin, Samir. "Le modèle théorétique d'accumulation et de développement dans le monde contemporain. La problématique de transition." *Tiers Monde* 52 (1972): 10-12.

Amin, Samir. "Underdevelopment and Dependence in Black Africa: Their Historical Origins and Contemporary Forms." *Social and Economic Studies* 22 (1980): 227-48.

Balachandran, P.K. "An Embattled Community: Asians in East Africa Today." *African Affairs* 80, no. 320 (July 1981), pp. 317-326.

Barker, David, and Ferguson, Alan. "The Craft Training Center as a Rural Mobilization Policy in Kenya." *Rural Africana* 12-13 (Winter-Spring 1981-82): 75-90.

Bernard, Frank E. "Meru District in the Kenyan Spatial Economy: 1890- 1950." In *The Spatial Structure of Development: A Study of Kenya*, pp. 264-290. Edited by R.A. Obudho and D.R.F. Taylor. Boulder, Colo: Westview Press, 1979.

Berry, Brian J.L. "Hierarchical Diffusion: The Basis of Developmental Filtering and Spread in a System of Growth Centers." In *Growth Centers in Regional Economic Development*. Edited by Niles Hansen. New York: Free Press, 1972.

Berry, Len. "Dynamics and Processes of Rural Change." In *Contemporary Africa: Geography and Change*, pp. 212-225. Edited by C. Gregory Knight and James L. Newman. Englewood Cliffs, N.J.: Prentice Hall, 1976.

Bienefield, M. "The Informal Sector and Peripheral Capitalism: The Case of Tanzania." *Bulletin of the Institute of Development Studies* 6, no. 3 (1975), pp. 53-73.

Bigsten, Arne. *Regional Inequality and Development: A Case Study of Kenya*. Farmborough: Gower Publishing, 1980.

Bohannan, P., and Dalton, G., eds. *Markets in Africa*. Evanston: Northwestern University Press, 1962.

Bromley, R.J. *Periodic Markets, Daily Markets and Fairs: A Bibliography*. Centre for Development Studies, Occasional Papers Series. Swansea: University College of Swansea, 1977.

Brookfield, Harold. *Interdependent Development*. London: Methuen, 1975.

Brookfield, Harold. "On One Geography and a Third World." *Institute of British Geographers, Transactions* 58 (1973): 1-20.

Browett, J.G. "On the Role of Geography in Development Geography." *Tijdschrift voor Economische en Sociale Geografie* 72, no. 3 (1981), pp. 155-161.

Brown, Lawrence A. *Innovation Diffusion: A New Perspective.* London and New York: Methuen, 1981.

Carr, J.L. "The Function and Development of Rural Market Systems, Murang'a District, Kenya." Cambridge, 1979. (Mimeographed.)

Chanler, W.A. *Through Jungle and Desert: Travels in Eastern Africa.* London: Macmillan, 1896.

Clark, N., et al. "Maket Raun: A Report to the Central Planning Office." Papua, New Guinea, 1971. (Mimeographed.)

Cleevely, D.D., and Walsham, G. "Modelling the Role of Telecommunications within Regions of Kenya." Cambridge: University of Cambridge Department of Engineering, 1981. (Mimeographed.)

Collier, Valerie G., and Rempel, Henry. "The Divergence of Private from Social Costs in Rural Urban Migration: A Case Study of Nairobi." In *Papers on the Kenyan Economy: Performance, Problems and Policies,* pp. 228-237. Edited by Tony Killick. Nairobi: Heinemann, 1981.

Colony and Protectorate of Kenya. *A Plan to Intensify the Development of African Agriculture in Kenya.* Nairobi: The Government Printer, 1954.

Coombs, Philip H., ed. *Meeting the Basic Needs of the Rural Poor: The Integrated Community-Based Approach.* Oxford: Pergamon Press, 1980.

Cowen, Michael. "Commodity Production in Kenya's Central Province." In *Rural Development in Tropical Africa,* pp. 121-142. Edited by Judith Heyer, Pepe Roberts, and Gavin Williams. London: Macmillan, 1981.

Curry, Robert L. Jr. "The Global Economy's Impact on Planning in Kenya and the Sudan." *Journal of African Studies* 9, no. 2 (Summer 1982), pp. 76-82.

Davis, J.T. "Development of the Small-farm Sector in Kenya, 1954-1972." *The Canadian Geographer* 21, no.1 (1977), pp. 32-58.

de Souza, Anthony R. "Commentary: Dialectic Development Geography." *Tijdschrift voor Economische en Sociale Geografie* 73, no. 2 (1982), pp. 122-128.

de Souza, Anthony R., and Porter, P.W. *The Underdevelopment and Modernization of the Third World.* Commission on College Geography, Resource Paper no. 28. Washington, D.C.: Association of American Geographers, 1974

Eighmy, T.H. "Rural Periodic Markets and the Extension of an Urban System: A Western Nigeria Example." *Economic Geography* 48, no. 3 (July 1972), pp. 299-315.

Elkan, W. "Circular Migration and the Growth of Towns in East Africa." *International Labor Review* 96 (1967): 581-589.

Elkan, W.; Ryan, T.C.; and Mukui, J.T. "The Economics of Shoe Shining in Nairobi." *African Affairs* 81, no. 323 (April 1982), pp. 247-256.

Ettema, W.A. "Geographers and Development." *Tijschrift voor Economische en Sociale Geografie* 70 (1979): 66-74.

Fei, J.C.H., and Ranis, G. *Development of the Labor Surplus Economy.* Homewood, Ill.: Irwin, 1964.

Frank, Andre G. *Capitalism and Underdevelopment in Latin America: Historical Studies in Chile and Brazil.* Revised ed. New York: Monthly Review Press, 1969.

Freeman, Donald B. *The Geography of Development and Modernization: A Survey of Present Trends and Future Prospects.* Discussion Paper no. 22. Toronto: York University, Department of Geography, 1979.

Freeman, Donald B. "Mobile Enterprises and Markets in Central Province, Kenya." *Geographical Review* 70, no. 1 (January 1980), pp. 36-49.

Freeman, Donald B., and Solberg, Birger. "Effects of Mill Location, Size, and Input Characteristics on the Economic Efficiency of Kenya's Forest Industries." *Tijdschrift voor Economische en Sociale Geografie* 69, no. 3 (1978). pp. 141-153.

Freeman, Donald B., and Norcliffe, Glen. "The Rural Nonfarm Sector: Development Opportunity or Employer of Last Resort?" *Ceres: The FAO Review on Agriculture and Development* 16, no. 1 (1983), pp. 28-34.

Freeman, Donald B., and Norcliffe, Glen. "Relations between the Rural Nonfarm and Small Farm Sector in Central Province, Kenya." *Tijdschrift voor Economische en Sociale Geografie* 75 (1983), pp. 61-73.

Freeman, Donald B., and Norcliffe, Glen. "The Rural Nonfarm Sector and the Development Process in Kenya." In *Planning African Development,* pp. 62-78. Edited by Glen Norcliffe and Tom Pinfold. Boulder and London: Westview Press and Croom Helm, 1981.

Freidmann, John. "A General Theory of Polarized Development." In *Growth Centers in Regional Economic Development.* Edited by Niles M. Hansen. New York: Free Press, 1972.

Friedmann, John, and Douglass, M. "Regional Planning and Development: The Agropolitan Approach." In *Growth Pole Strategy and Regional Development Planning in Asia,* pp. 333-387. Nagoya: United Nations Centre for Regional Development, 1976.

Friedmann, John, and Weaver, Clyde. *Territory and Function: The Evolution of Regional Planning.* Berkeley and Los Angeles: University of California Press, 1979.

Frontera, Anne E. *Persistence and Change: A History of Taveta.* Waltham, Mass.: Brandeis University, African Studies Association, 1978.

Gaile, Gary L. "Processes Affecting the Spatial Pattern of Rural-Urban Development in Kenya." *African Studies Review* 19, no. 3 (December 1976), pp. 1-16.

Gauhar, Altaf. "What Is Wrong with Basic Needs?" Editorial. *Third World Quarterly* 4, no. 3 (July 1982), pp. xxi-xxiii.

Ghai, D.; Thorbecke, E.; and Godfrey, M. "Alleviating Poverty and Meeting Basic Human Needs in Kenya: Report of an ILO Consultancy Mission." Nairobi, 1977. (Mimeographed).

Godfrey, Martin. "Basic Needs and Planning in Kenya." In *Models, Planning and Basic Needs.* Edited by S. Cole and H. Lucas. Oxford: Pergamon Press, 1979.

Godfrey, Martin, and Langdon, Steven. "Partners in Underdevelopment? The Transnationalization Thesis in a Kenyan Context." In *Transnational Capitalism and National Development*, pp. 261-288. Edited by José Villamil. Sussex: Harvester Press, 1979.

Good, Charles M. *Rural Markets and Trade in East Africa*. Research Paper no. 128. Chicago: University of Chicago, Department of Geography, 1970.

Good, Charles M. *Market Development in Traditionally Marketless Societies: A Perspective on East Africa*. Centre for International Studies, Paper no. 12 (Africa Series). Columbus, Ohio: Ohio State University, 1971.

Good, Charles M. "Markets and Marketing Systems." In *Contemporary Africa: Geography and Change*, pp. 364-386. Edited by C.G. Knight and J.L. Newman. Englewood Cliffs, N.J.: Prentice Hall, 1976.

Goodenough, Stephanie. *Values, Relevance and Ideology in Third World Geography*. Milton Keynes: Open University Press, 1977.

Gould, Peter. *Spatial Diffusion*. Resource Paper Series. Washington: Association of American Geographers, 1969.

Gould, Peter. "Tanzania, 1920-1963: The Spatial Impress of the Modernization Process." In *Contemporary Africa: Geography and Change*, pp. 423-438. Edited by C.G. Knight and J.L. Newman. Englewood Cliffs, N.J.: Prentice Hall, 1976.

Government of Kenya. "The Strategy of the Fourth Development Plan 1979-83." In *Papers on the Kenyan Economy: Performance, Problems and Policies*, pp. 90-96. Edited by Tony Killick. Nairobi: Heinemann, 1981.

Harris, John R., and Todaro, Michael P. "Migration, Unemployment and Development: A Two-Sector Analysis." *American Economic Review* 55 (1970): 126-41.

Hazlewood, Arthur. *The Economy of Kenya: The Kenyatta Era*. London: Oxford University Press, 1979.

Henkel, Reinhard. *Central Places in Western Kenya*. Geographic Institute Publication no. 54. Heidelberg: University of Heidelberg, 1979.

Heyer, Judith. "Agricultural Development Policy in Kenya from the Colonial Period to 1975." In *Rural Development in Tropical Africa*, pp. 90-120. Edited by J. Heyer, P. Roberts, and G. Williams. London: Macmillan, 1981.

Heyer, Judith; Ireri, D.; and Moris, L. *Rural Development in Kenya*. Nairobi: East African Publishing House, 1971.

Heyer, Judith; Roberts, Pepe; and Williams, Gavin. "Rural Development." In *Rural Development in Tropical Africa*, pp. 1-15. Edited by Judith Heyer, Pepe Roberts, and Gavin Williams London: Macmillan, 1981.

Higgins, Benjamin. *Economic Development*. Revised ed. New York: W.W. Norton, 1968.

Hill, Polly, and Smith, Robert H.T. "The Spatial and Temporal Synchronization of Periodic Markets: Evidence from Four Emirates in Northern Nigeria." *Economic Geography* 48, no. 3 (July 1972), pp. 345-355.

Hodder, B.W. "Markets in Yorubaland." In *Markets in West Africa:
Studies of Markets and Trade among the Yoruba and Ido*. Edited
by B.W. Hodder and U.I. Ukwu. Ibadan: Ibadan University Press,
1969.

Hodder, B.W. "The Distribution of Markets in Yorubaland." *Scottish
Geographical Magazine* 81 (1965): 48-58.

House, William J. "Nairobi's Informal Sector: An Exploratory
Study." In *Papers on the Kenyan Economy: Performance,
Problems and Policies*, pp. 357-368. Edited by T. Killick.
Nairobi: Heinemann, 1981.

House, William J.; and Killick, Tony. "Inequality and Poverty in
the Rural Economy, and the Influence of Some Aspects of
Policy." In *Papers on the Kenyan Economy: Performance,
Problems and Policies*, pp. 157-179. Edited by T. Killick.
Nairobi: Heinemann, 1981.

Hoyle, B.S., ed. *Spatial Aspects of Development*. London: John
Wiley, 1974.

International Labour Office. *Employment, Incomes and Equality: A
Strategy for Increasing Productive Employment in Kenya*.
Geneva: ILO Publications, 1972.

International Labour Office, World Employment Programme. *Programme
on Rural Industrialization, Rural Nonfarm Technology and
Employment*. Geneva: ILO, 1978.

Inukai, Ichirou. "Rural Industrialization: A Country Study, Kenya."
Nairobi: University of Nairobi, Department of Economics, 1972.
(Mimeographed).

Inukai, Ichirou. "African Socialism and Agricultural Development
Strategy: A Comparative Study of Kenya and Tanzania." *The
Developing Economies* 12, no. 1 (March 1974), pp. 3-22.

Johnson, E.A.J. *The Organization of Space in Developing Countries*.
Cambridge, Mass.: Harvard University Press, 1970.

Johnson, G.E., and Whitelaw, W.E. "Urban-Rural Income Transfers in
Kenya: An Estimated Remittance Function." *Economic Development
and Cultural Change* 22 (1974): 473-79.

Killick, Tony., ed. *Papers on the Kenyan Economy: Performance,
Problems and Policies*. Nairobi: Heinemann, 1981.

Killick, Tony. "The Possibilities of Development Planning." *Oxford
Economic Papers* 28 (1976): 161-183.

Kaplinsky, Raphael, ed. *Readings on the Multinational Corporation
in Kenya*. Nairobi: Oxford University Press, 1978.

Kimani, S., and Taylor, D.R.F. *Growth Centres and Rural
Development*. Thika: Maxim Printers, 1973. King, Kenneth. *The
African Artisan: Education and the Informal Sector in Kenya*.
London: Heinemann, 1977.

Kitching, G.N. *Social and Economic Inequality in Rural East Africa:
The Present as a Clue to the Past*. Centre for Development
Studies, Occasional Paper Series. Swansea: University College
of Swansea, 1977.

Knight, C. Gregory. "Prospects for Peasant Agriculture." In
Contemporary Africa: Geography and Change, pp. 195-211.
Edited by C. Gregory Knight and James L. Newman. Englewood
Cliffs, N.J.: Prentice Hall, 1976.

Lamphear, John. "The Kamba and the Northern Mrima Coast." In *Pre-Colonial African Trade,* pp. 75-102. Edited by R. Gray and D. Birmingham. London: Oxford University Press, 1970.

Lewis, J. "Ideology and the Geography of Development." Paper prepared for the Anglo-French Symposium on Ideology and Geography, March 23-25, 1979.

Lewis, W.A. "Economic Development with Unlimited Supplies of Labour." In *The Economics of Underdevelopment.* Edited by A.N. Agarwala and S.P. Singh. New York: Oxford University Press, 1958.

Leys, Colin. "Interpreting African Underdevelopment: Reflections on the ILO Report on Employment, Incomes and Equality in Kenya." *African Affairs* 73 (October 1973): 419-429.

Leys, Colin. *Underdevelopment in Kenya: The Political Economy of Neo-Colonialism.* London: Heinemann. 1975.

Leys, Colin. "Capital Accumulation, Class Formation and Dependency: The Significance of the Kenyan Case." *The Socialist Register* (1978): 241-266.

Logan, M.I. "The Development Process in the Less Developed Countries." *Australian Geographer* 12 (1972): 146-53.

Mabogunje, Akin L. *The Development Process: A Spatial Perspective.* London: Hutchinson & Co., University Library for Africa, 1980.

Marris, R., and Somerset, A. *African Businessmen.* Nairobi: East African Publishing House, 1971.

McGee, T.G., and Yeung, Yue-Man. *Hawkers in Southeast Asia: Planning for the Bazaar Economy.* Ottawa: International Development Research Centre, 1977.

McKay, J. "A Review of Rural Settlement Studies for Tanzania." *East African Geographical Review* 6 (1968): 37-49.

McMaster, David N. "Rural Development and Economic Growth: Kenya." *Focus* 25, no. 5 (January-February 1975), pp. 8-15.

Mehretu, Assefa, and Campbell, David J. "Regional Planning for Small Communities in Rural Africa: A Critical Survey." *Rural Africana* 12-13 (Winter-Spring 1981-82): 91-110.

Meunch, Louis H. "A Final Demand Approach to the Informal Sector and Implications for Public Policies." In *The Informal Sector in Kenya,* pp. 5-34. Edited by S.B. Westley and D. Kabagambe. Institute for Development Studies, Occasional Paper no. 25. Nairobi: University of Nairobi, 1977.

Moser, Carolyn O.M. "Informal Sector or Petty Commodity Production: Dualism or Dependence in Urban Development." *World Development* 6 (1978): 1041-64.

Mosley, Paul. "Kenya in the 1970's: A Review Article." *African Affairs* 81, no. 323 (April 1982), pp. 271-77.

Myint, H. "The Demand Approach to Economic Development." *Review of Economic Studies* 27 (1970): 124-132.

Myrdal, Gunnar. *Asian Drama: An Inquiry into the Poverty of Nations.* 2 vols. New York: Pantheon Press, 1968.

Norcliffe, Glen B., and Freeman, Donald B. "Nonfarm Activities in Market Centres of Central Province, Kenya." *Canadian Journal of African Studies* 14 (1980): 503-517.

Norcliffe, Glen B.; Freeman, D.B.; and Miles, N.J.O. *Policies for Rural Industrialization in Kenya.* Rural Industrialization Project, Working Paper no. 1. Geneva: International Labour Office, 1980.

Norcliffe, Glen B., and Pinfold, Tom, ed. *Planning African Development.* Boulder, Colo. and London: Westview and Croom Helm, 1981.

North, Douglass C. "Location Theory and Economic Growth." In *Regional Development and Planning,* pp. 240-255. Edited by J. Friedmann and W. Alonso. Cambridge, Mass: M.I.T. Press, 1964.

Nurkse, Ragnar. *Problems of Capital Formation in Underdeveloped Countries.* Oxford: Blackwell, 1957.

Obudho, R.A. "Temporal Periodicity and Locational Spacing of Periodic and Daily Markets in Kenya." *Cahiers d'etudes africaines* 16 (1977): 553-66.

Otieza, Enrique. "Collective Self-Reliance: Some Old and New Issues." In *Transnational Capitalism and National Development,* pp. 298-306. Edited by José Villamil. Sussex: The Harvester Press, 1979.

Padmore, George. *How Britain Rules Africa.* New York: Lothrop, Lee and Shepherd, 1936.

Palma, Gabriel. "Dependency: A Formal Theory of Underdevelopment or a Methodology for the Analysis of Concrete Situations of Underdevelopment?" *World Development* 6 (1978): 881-924.

Pandit, S., ed. *Asians in East and Central Africa.* Nairobi: Panco Publications, 1963.

Peattie, Lisa R. "Anthropological Perspectives on the Concepts of Dualism, the Informal Sector, and Marginality in Developing Urban Economies." *International Regional Science Review* 5, no. 1 (1980), pp. 1-31.

Peet, Richard. "Inequality and Poverty: A Marxist-Geographic Theory." *Annals of the Association of American Geographers* 65, no. 4 (1975), pp. 564-71.

Pinfold, Tom, and Norcliffe, Glen, eds. *Development Planning in Kenya.* Geographical Monographs, no. 9. Toronto: York University, Atkinson College, 1980.

Porter, Philip W. "Climate and Agriculture in East Africa." In *Contemporary Africa: Geography and Change,* pp. 112-139. Edited by C. Gregory Knight and James L. Newman. Englewood Cliffs, N.J.: Prentice Hall, 1976.

Pratt, D.J., and Gwynne, M.D., eds. *Rangeland Management and Ecology in East Africa.* London: Hodder and Stoughton, 1977.

Rempel, Henry. *The Role of Rural-urban Migration in the Urbanization and Economic Development Occurring in Kenya.* Research Memorandum. Laxenberg, Austria: International Institute for Applied Systems Analysis, 1978.

Rempel, Henry, and House, William J. *The Kenya Employment Problem: An Analysis of the Modern Sector Labour Market.* Nairobi: Oxford University Press, 1978.

Republic of Kenya. *Development Plan 1974-78, Vol. I.* Nairobi: Government Printer, 1974.

Republic of Kenya. *On Economic Prospects and Policies.* Sessional Paper no. 4. Nairobi: Government Printer, 1975.

Republic of Kenya, Central Bureau of Statistics. *Integrated Survey 1974-75*. Nairobi: Ministry of Finance and Planning, 1977.

Republic of Kenya, Ministry of Economic Planning and Development. "Alleviating Poverty and Meeting Basic Human Needs in Kenya." 1977. (Mimeographed.)

Republic of Kenya, Central Bureau of Statistics. "Nonfarm Activities in Rural Kenyan Households." *Social Perspectives* 2, no. 2 (1977), 12 pp.

Republic of Kenya, Central Bureau of Statistics. "Urban Purchasing Patterns." *Social Perspectives* 3, no. 1 (1978), 12 pp.

Republic of Kenya, Central Bureau of Statistics. *Economic Survey 1980*. Nairobi: Government Printer, 1980.

Republic of Kenya. Central Bureau of Statistics. *Social Accounting Matrix 1976 (Revised)*. Nairobi: Government Printer, 1981.

Richardson, H.W. "Growth Centers, Rural Development and National Urban Policy: A Defence." *International Regional Science Review* 3, no. 2 (1978), pp. 133-152.

Riddell, J. Barry. "Review Essay: The Geography Of Modernization in Africa: A Re-examination." *The Canadian Geographer* 25, no. 3 (Autumn 1981), pp. 290-299.

Riddell, J. Barry. "Modernization in Sierra Leone." In *Contemporary Africa: Geography and Change*, pp. 393-407. Edited by C. Gregory Knight and James L. Newman. Englewood Cliffs, N.J.: Prentice Hall, 1976.

Rimmer, Peter, and Forbes, Dean. "Under-development Theory: A Geographical Review." *Australian Geographer* 15, no. 4 (November 1982), pp. 197-210.

Rondinelli, Dennis, and Ruddle, Kenneth. *Urbanization and Rural Development: A Spatial Policy for Equitable Growth*. New York: Praeger, 1978.

Rostow, Walt. *Stages of Economic Growth: A Non-Communist Manifesto*. Cambridge: University Press, 1960.

Rostow, Walt. "A Fresh Start for the Americas." *The Americas* 31, no. 2 (February 1979), pp. 39-44.

Sachs, Ignacy. "Ecodevelopment." *Ceres: The FAO Review on Agriculture and Development* 44, no. 6 (1974), pp. 8-12.

Seers, Dudley. "Patterns of Dependence." In *Transnational Capitalism and National Development*, pp. 95-114. Edited by José Villamil. Sussex: Harvester Press, 1979.

Senghaas-Knobloch, E. "Informal Sector and Peripheral Capitalism: Critique of a Prevailing Concept of Development." *Manpower and Unemployment Research* 10, no. 2 (November 1977), pp. 3-24.

Sethuraman, S.V. "Survey Instrument for a Study of the Urban Informal Sector: The Case of Jakarta." Geneva: International Labour Office, 1975. (Mimeographed).

Sharpley, Jennifer. "Resource Transfers between the Agricultural and Nonagricultural Sectors: 1964-1977." In *Papers on the Kenyan Economy: Performance, Problems and Policies*, pp. 311-319. Edited by Tony Killick. Nairobi: Heinemann, (1981).

Skinner, G.W. "Marketing and Social Structure in Rural China, Part I." *Journal of Asian Studies* 24 (1964): 3-43.

Slater, David. "Geography and Underdevelopment." *Antipode* 5, no. 3 (1973), pp. 21-33.

Smith, Neil. "Theories of Underdevelopment: A Response to Reitsma." *Professional Geographer* 34, no. 3 (1982), pp. 332-36.

Smith, R.H.T., and Hay, A.M. "A Theory of the Spatial Structure of Internal Trade in Underdeveloped Countries." *Geographical Analysis* 1 (1969): 121-36.

Sorrenson, M.P.K. *Land Reform in the Kikuyu Country.* Nairobi: Oxford University Press, 1967.

Soja, Edward. "The Geography of Modernization--A Radical Reappraisal." In *The Spatial Structure of Development: A Study of Kenya,* pp. 28-45. Edited by R.A. Obudho and D.R.F. Taylor. Boulder, Colo.: Westview Press, 1979.

Soja, Edward. *The Geography of Modernization in Kenya.* Syracuse: Syracuse University Press, 1968.

Spencer, I.G.R. "The First Assault on Indian Ascendancy: Indian Traders in the Kenya Reserves 1895-1929." *African Affairs* 80, no. 320 (July 1981), pp. 327-44.

Steel, William F. *Small-scale Employment and Production in Developing Countries: Evidence from Ghana.* New York: Praeger, 1977.

Stine, J.H. "Temporal Aspects of Tertiary Production Elements in Korea." In *Urban System and Economic Development,* pp. 68-88. Edited by Forrest R. Pitts. Eugene, Oregon: University of Oregon, School of Business Administration, 1962.

Stohr, W., and Palme, H. "Center-Periphery Development Alternatives and the Applicability to Rural Areas in Developing Countries." Paper prepared for the ASA/LASA Joint Meetings, Houston, Texas, September 1977.

Stohr, W., and Taylor, D.R.F., eds. *Development from Above or Below?* New York: Wiley and Sons, 1981.

Streeten, Paul. *The Distinctive Features of a Basic Needs Approach to Development.* Washington, D.C.: World Bank, Policy Planning and Program Review Department, 1977. (Mimeographed.)

Swainson, Nicola. "State and Economy in Post-Colonial Kenya, 1963-1978." *Review Canadienne des Études Africaines/Canadian Journal of African Studies* 12, no. 3 (1978), pp. 357-81.

Szentes, Tamas. *The Political Economy of Underdevelopment.* Budapest: Akademiai Kiado, 1971.

Taylor, D.R.F. "Spatial Aspects of the Development Process." In *The Spatial Structure of Development. A Study of Kenya,* pp. 1-27. Edited by R.A. Obudho and D.R.F. Taylor. Boulder, Colo.: Westview Press, 1979.

Taylor, D.R.F. "The Internal Trade of Fort Hall District, Kenya." *Canadian Journal of African Studies* 1 (1967): 111-22.

Taylor, D.R.F. "The Role of the Smaller Urban Place in Development: A Case Study from Kenya." Ottawa: Carleton University, Department of Geography and School of International Affairs, undated. (Mimeographed.)

Taylor, D.R.F. "Agricultural Change in Kikuyuland." In *Environment and Land Use in Africa.* Edited by Thomas and Whittington. London, 1969.

Todaro, Michael P. "A Model of Labor Migration and Urban Unemployment in Less Developed Countries." *American Economic Review* 59 (1969): 138-48.

Valenzuela, J. Samuel, and Valenzuela, Arturo. "Modernization and Dependence: Alternative Perspectives in the Study of Latin American Underdevelopment." In *Transnational Capitalism and National Development,* pp. 31-66. Edited by José Villamil. Sussex: The Harvester Press, 1979.

Villamil, José, ed. *Transnational Capitalism and National Development.* Sussex: The Harvester Press, 1979.

Walden, Thorn. "Entrepreneurial Illiquidity Preference and the African Extended Family." In *Development Planning in Kenya: Essays on the Planning Process and Policy Issues,* pp. 119-40. Edited by T. Pinfold and G. Norcliffe. Department of Geography, Geographical Monographs, no. 9. Toronto: York University, Atkinson College, 1980.

Ward, R.G. et al. *Growth Centres and Area Improvement in the Eastern Highland District: A Report to the Central Planning Office, Papua-New Guinea.* Research School of Pacific Studies. Canberra: Australian National University, 1974.

Wescott, Clay G. "Industrial Policy: A Case Study of Incentives for Industrial Dispersion." In *Papers on the Kenyan Economy: Performance, Problems and Policies,* pp. 346-56. Edited by Tony Killick. Nairobi: Heinemann, 1981.

Wescott, Clay, and Glen Norcliffe. "Towards a Locational Policy for Manufacturing Industry in Kenya." In *Planning African Development,* pp. 79-109. Edited by Glen Norcliffe and Tom Pinfold. Boulder, Colo. and London: Westview and Croom Helm, 1981.

Westley, Sidney, and Kabagambe, Dennis, eds. *The Informal Sector in Kenya.* Occasional Paper no. 25. Nairobi: University of Nairobi, January 1978.

Wood, L.J. "The Functional Structure of a Rural Market System." *Geografiska Annaler,* Series B 57, no. 2 (1975), pp. 109-118.

Wood, L.J. "Population Density and Rural Market Provision." *Cahiers d'études Africaines* 14 (1974): 715-26.

World Bank. *Kenya: Into the Second Decade.* Baltimore: Johns Hopkins Press, for the World Bank, 1975.

World Bank. *World Development Report 1981.* Washington, D.C.: The World Bank, August 1981.

THE UNIVERSITY OF CHICAGO
DEPARTMENT OF GEOGRAPHY
RESEARCH PAPERS (Lithographed, 6×9 inches)

LIST OF TITLES IN PRINT

133. SCHWIND, PAUL J. *Migration and Regional Development in the United States.* 1971. 170 p.

134. PYLE, GERALD F. *Heart Disease, Cancer and Stroke in Chicago: A Geographical Analysis with Facilities, Plans for 1980.* 1971. 292 p.

135. JOHNSON, JAMES F. *Renovated Waste Water: An Alternative Source of Municipal Water Supply in the United States.* 1971. 155 p.

136. BUTZER, KARL W. *Recent History of an Ethiopian Delta: The Omo River and the Level of Lake Rudolf.* 1971. 184 p.

139. MCMANIS, DOUGLAS R. *European Impressions of the New England Coast, 1497–1620.* 1972. 147 p.

140. COHEN, YEHOSHUA S. *Diffusion of an Innovation in an Urban System: The Spread of Planned Regional Shopping Centers in the United States, 1949–1968,* 1972. 136 p.

141. MITCHELL, NORA. *The Indian Hill-Station: Kodaikanal.* 1972. 199 p.

142. PLATT, RUTHERFORD H. *The Open Space Decision Process: Spatial Allocation of Costs and Benefits.* 1972. 189 p.

143. GOLANT, STEPHEN M. *The Residential Location and Spatial Behavior of the Elderly: A Canadian Example.* 1972. 226 p.

144. PANNELL, CLIFTON W. *T'ai-chung, T'ai-wan: Structure and Function.* 1973. 200 p.

145. LANKFORD, PHILIP M. *Regional Incomes in the United States, 1929–1967: Level, Distribution, Stability, and Growth.* 1972. 137 p.

146. FREEMAN, DONALD B. *International Trade, Migration, and Capital Flows: A Quantitative Analysis of Spatial Economic Interaction.* 1973. 201 p.

147. MYERS, SARAH K. *Language Shift Among Migrants to Lima, Peru.* 1973. 203 p.

148. JOHNSON, DOUGLAS L. *Jabal al-Akhdar, Cyrenaica: An Historical Geography of Settlement and Livelihood.* 1973. 240 p.

149. YEUNG, YUE-MAN. *National Development Policy and Urban Transformation in Singapore: A Study of Public Housing and the Marketing System.* 1973. 204 p.

150. HALL, FRED L. *Location Criteria for High Schools: Student Transportation and Racial Integration.* 1973. 156 p.

151. ROSENBERG, TERRY J. *Residence, Employment, and Mobility of Puerto Ricans in New York City.* 1974. 230 p.

152. MIKESELL, MARVIN W., editor. *Geographers Abroad: Essays on the Problems and Prospects of Research in Foreign Areas.* 1973. 296 p.

153. OSBORN, JAMES F. *Area, Development Policy, and the Middle City in Malaysia.* 1974. 291 p.

154. WACHT, WALTER F. *The Domestic Air Transportation Network of the United States.* 1974. 98 p.

155. BERRY, BRIAN J. L., et al. *Land Use, Urban Form and Environmental Quality.* 1974. 440 p.

156. MITCHELL, JAMES K. *Community Response to Coastal Erosion: Individual and Collective Adjustments to Hazard on the Atlantic Shore.* 1974. 209 p.

157. COOK, GILLIAN P. *Spatial Dynamics of Business Growth in the Witwatersrand.* 1975. 144 p.

159. PYLE, GERALD F. et al. *The Spatial Dynamics of Crime.* 1974. 221 p.

160. MEYER, JUDITH W. *Diffusion of an American Montessori Education.* 1975. 97 p.

161. SCHMID, JAMES A. *Urban Vegetation: A Review and Chicago Case Study.* 1975. 266 p.

162. LAMB, RICHARD F. *Metropolitan Impacts on Rural America.* 1975. 196 p.

163. FEDOR, THOMAS STANLEY. *Patterns of Urban Growth in the Russian Empire during the Nineteenth Century.* 1975. 245 p.

164. HARRIS, CHAUNCY D. *Guide to Geographical Bibliographies and Reference Works in Russian or on the Soviet Union.* 1975. 478 p.

165. JONES, DONALD W. *Migration and Urban Unemployment in Dualistic Economic Development.* 1975. 174 p.

166. BEDNARZ, ROBERT S. *The Effect of Air Pollution on Property Value in Chicago.* 1975. 111 p.

167. HANNEMANN, MANFRED. *The Diffusion of the Reformation in Southwestern Germany, 1518–1534.* 1975. 248 p.

168. SUBLETT, MICHAEL D. *Farmers on the Road. Interfarm Migration and the Farming of Noncontiguous Lands in Three Midwestern Townships. 1939–1969.* 1975. 228 pp.

169. STETZER, DONALD FOSTER. *Special Districts in Cook County: Toward a Geography of Local Government.* 1975. 189 pp.

170. EARLE, CARVILLE V. *The Evolution of a Tidewater Settlement System: All Hallow's Parish, Maryland, 1650–1783.* 1975. 249 pp.

171. SPODEK, HOWARD. *Urban-Rural Integration in Regional Development: A Case Study of Saurashtra, India—1800–1960.* 1976. 156 pp.

172. COHEN, YEHOSHUA S. and BERRY, BRIAN J. L. *Spatial Components of Manufacturing Change.* 1975. 272 pp.

173. HAYES, CHARLES R. *The Dispersed City: The Case of Piedmont, North Carolina.* 1976. 169 pp.

174. CARGO, DOUGLAS B. *Solid Wastes: Factors Influencing Generation Rates.* 1977. 112 pp.

175. GILLARD, QUENTIN. *Incomes and Accessibility. Metropolitan Labor Force Participation, Commuting, and Income Differentials in the United States, 1960–1970.* 1977. 140 pp.

176. MORGAN, DAVID J. *Patterns of Population Distribution: A Residential Preference Model and Its Dynamic.* 1978. 216 pp.

177. STOKES, HOUSTON H.; JONES, DONALD W. and NEUBURGER, HUGH M. *Unemployment and Adjustment in the Labor Market: A Comparison between the Regional and National Responses.* 1975. 135 pp.

179. HARRIS, CHAUNCY D. *Bibliography of Geography. Part I. Introduction to General Aids.* 1976. 288 pp.

180. CARR, CLAUDIA J. *Pastoralism in Crisis. The Dasanetch and their Ethiopian Lands.* 1977. 339 pp.

181. GOODWIN, GARY C. *Cherokees in Transition: A Study of Changing Culture and Environment Prior to 1775.* 1977. 221 pp.

182. KNIGHT, DAVID B. *A Capital for Canada: Conflict and Compromise in the Nineteenth Century.* 1977. 359 pp.

183. HAIGH, MARTIN J. *The Evolution of Slopes on Artificial Landforms: Blaenavon, Gwent.* 1978. 311 pp.

184. FINK, L. DEE. *Listening to the Learner. An Exploratory Study of Personal Meaning in College Geography Courses.* 1977. 200 pp.

185. HELGREN, DAVID M. *Rivers of Diamonds: An Alluvial History of the Lower Vaal Basin.* 1979. 399 pp.

186. BUTZER, KARL W., editor. *Dimensions of Human Geography: Essays on Some Familiar and Neglected Themes.* 1978. 201 pp.

187. MITSUHASHI, SETSUKO. *Japanese Commodity Flows.* 1978. 185 pp.

188. CARIS, SUSAN L. *Community Attitudes toward Pollution.* 1978. 226 pp.

189. REES, PHILIP M. *Residential Patterns in American Cities, 1960.* 1979. 424 pp.

190. KANNE, EDWARD A. *Fresh Food for Nicosia.* 1979. 116 pp.

192. KIRCHNER, JOHN A. *Sugar and Seasonal Labor Migration: The Case of Tucumán, Argentina.* 1980. 158 pp.

193. HARRIS, CHAUNCY D. and FELLMANN, JEROME D. *International List of Geographical Serials, Third Edition, 1980.* 1980. 457 p.

194. HARRIS, CHAUNCY D. *Annotated World List of Selected Current Geographical Serials, Fourth, Edition. 1980.* 1980. 165 p.

195. LEUNG, CHI-KEUNG. *China: Railway Patterns and National Goals.* 1980. 235 p.

196. LEUNG, CHI-KEUNG and GINSBURG, NORTON S., eds. *China: Urbanization and National Development.* 1980. 280 p.

197. DAICHES, SOL. *People in Distress: A Geographical Perspective on Psychological Well-being.* 1981. 199 p.

198. JOHNSON, JOSEPH T. *Location and Trade Theory: Industrial Location, Comparative Advantage, and the Geographic Pattern of Production in the United States.* 1981. 107 p.

199-200. STEVENSON, ARTHUR J. *The New York-Newark Air Freight System.* 1982. 440 p.

201. LICATE, JACK A. *Creation of a Mexican Landscape: Territorial Organization and Settlement in the Eastern Puebla Basin, 1520–1605.* 1981. 143 p.

202. RUDZITIS, GUNDARS. *Residential Location Determinants of the Older Population.* 1982. 117 p.

203. LIANG, ERNEST P. *China: Railways and Agricultural Development, 1875–1935.* 1982. 186 p.

204. DAHMANN, DONALD C. *Locals and Cosmopolitans: Patterns of Spatial Mobility during the Transition from Youth to Early Adulthood.* 1982. 146 p.

205. FOOTE, KENNETH E. *Color in Public Spaces: Toward a Communication-Based Theory of the Urban Built Environment.* 1983. 153 p.

206. HARRIS, CHAUNCY D. *Bibliography of Geography. Part II: Regional. Vol. 1. The United States of America.* 1984. 178 p.

207-208. WHEATLEY, PAUL. *Nāgara and Commandery: Origins of the Southeast Asian Urban Traditions.* 1983. 473 p.

209. SAARINEN, THOMAS F.; SEAMON, DAVID; and SELL, JAMES L., eds. *Environmental Perception and Behavior: An Inventory and Prospect.* 1984. 263 p.

210. WESCOAT, JAMES L., JR. *Integrated Water Development: Water Use and Conservation Practice in Western Colorado.* 1984. 239 p.

211. DEMKO, GEORGE J., and FUCHS, ROLAND J., eds. *Geographical Studies on the Soviet Union: Essays in Honor of Chauncy D. Harris.* 1984. 294 p.

213. EDMONDS, RICHARD L. *Northern Frontiers of Qing China and Tokugawa Japan: A Comparative Study of Frontier Policy.* 1985. 155 p.

214. FREEMAN, DONALD B., and NORCLIFFE, GLEN B. *Rural Enterprise in Kenya: Development and Spatial Organization of the Nonfarm Sector.* 1985. 180 p.

215. COHEN, YEHOSHUA S., and SHINAR, AMNON. *Neighborhoods and Friendship Networks: A Study of Three Residential Neighborhoods in Jerusalem.* 1985. 129 p.